framing

A complete introduction to the craft of framing

Eamon Toscano

Conceived and edited by
William and Shirley Sayles

Evans Brothers Limited London

Foreword

The craft of picture framing is one that I have been deeply committed to and involved in ever since my father brought me, as a child, into his shop. Such involvement, enjoying as it does a symbiotic relationship with art and painting, has brought me together with the artist as well as with the collector and decorator. The creative challenge for one interested in framing is therefore always present, and here lies the excitement and gratification of this craft. For the character of the art, the setting that will surround it, and the fashion of the day all need to be understood and considered when planning the frame. This involves such decisions as style of moulding, type of finish, the nature and purpose of the mount, and the suitability of a mount or liner – all considerations for the total enhancement and presentation of the picture.

In this book, Eamon Toscano, an experienced and practising craftsman, covers all these considerations clearly and in a well-organized manner. All the basic information for making picture frames is here, together with numerous examples of framed photographs, watercolours, prints, gouaches, needlework, oil paintings and others.

For those who are interested in picture framing as a profession, this book offers information not otherwise available except through direct apprentice-ship. For those who are interested in making their own frames, this book supplies directions pertinent to their needs. For those who would like to be knowledgeable when discussing their framing needs with a professional framer, this book is a must.

Marvin Pocker

This case-bound edition first published in Great Britain 1973 by Evans Brothers Limited, Montague House, Russell Square, London, W.C.1.
First British edition published 1972 by Pan Books Ltd.

© Western Publishing Co. Inc. 1971

Printed in Italy by Arnoldo Mondadori Editore, Verona
ISBN 0 237 44737 1

PRA 3392

Contents

ACKNOWLEDGEMENT

Among those who have assisted in the preparation
of this book, special thanks are due to:
   Remo Cosentino, *Design and Production*
   Stephen Manville, *Photography*

Introduction

It is not unusual to see a painting today that, aesthetically, does not require a frame. However, every picture requires a support if it is to be hung, and most require a glass facing for protection. The frames themselves, reflecting as they do the new simplicity in art, provide a happy opportunity for the individual craftsman since the design and construction of frames is well suited to home production.

Making frames at home is very much of a reality; the same materials used by the professional are available to the beginner at whatever quantity required; the tools are basic and familiar, simple to use, easy to obtain, and nominal in price; the techniques can be mastered quickly and give full opportunity for creativity. So long as you are careful, and conscientious in your workmanship, you can make a frame at home which will be equal in quality to one in a picture-framing shop, yet more gratifying because you created it.

WHY FRAME. Protection and presentation are the two main functions of the picture frame. If you own an object for which you feel joy and pride—like a photograph or a diploma or some treasured memento—it probably has value for you, and you don't want it damaged. Or you may have purchased an unframed painting on canvas at a street sale or a primitive at an auction, or a watercolour or print. Or perhaps you have cut a picture out of a magazine, or have a poster or map that you bought ready for framing. No matter what it is, framing will protect it as well as help show it off handsomely.

SOME POSSIBILITIES. You can work with frames alone or in combination with mats or mounts, either plain or fabric-covered. You can enjoy the tactile experience of working with wood moulding, exploring its grain and feeling its texture. You may decide that just a wax or stain finish is necessary to accentuate its handsomeness. Or you may choose another method, one of a variety, for finishing the frame. You can also frame temporarily by using various coloured tapes to bind the edges of the glass and simulate a frame while protecting its contents. This is known as passe partout. In all of this you need only to be led by your imagination, the requirements of the artwork, and those of its surroundings.

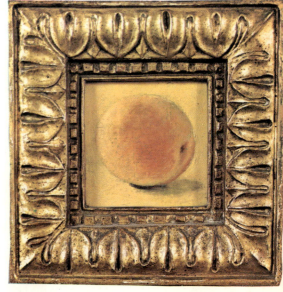

"Peach," by Elsie Manville. Oil. A frame can impart elegance to a simple subject. Hand-carved basswood with gold leaf on gesso, 279 mm (11 in.) square

(Facing page) "Guest Room," by Elsie Manville. Oil. Hand-carved French Provincial style moulding of waxed wormy chestnut. Frame size 916 mm x 610 mm (24 in. x 36 in.), moulding 50 mm (3 in.), with linen liner

SOME BACKGROUND. As styles in art change, so do the frames that surround them. During the latter part of the 19th century, a reaction set in against the brightly gilded frames which had been the style for so long. Simpler frames replaced the ribbons, flutes, and beads of historical carvings; and burlap, textured gesso, and paint replaced the gold leafing. These frames were frequently finished by the artist in an attempt to unify frame and painting by repeating, on the frame, motifs in the art. Wood finishes came into vogue in the 1930s when wormy chestnut and driftwood mouldings were introduced. The grain itself became important. To this day that of walnut remains one of the most widely appreciated.

Paintings as we know them–that is, as independent, integral, movable works of art–became prominent in the 13th century. Painting and frame were developed from the same wood panel. A surface for the painting was hollowed out of the wood; the frame was formed by the panel edges which were left at their original levels. Before long, painted wings were attached to the panels to form triptyches. This concept of multiple panels developed into the intricate altar-pieces of the 14th and 15th centuries; they were elaborate, primarily architectural units that often rose as high as fifteen feet. Requiring the talents of master craftsmen because of their complexity, they were, as a result, outstanding for their workmanship and beauty.

Fifteenth-century Italy popularized the use of mouldings, and by the time Columbus discovered America, mouldings were the most prevalent method of framing pictures. Those involved in the production of picture frames no longer had to concern themselves with structures that were primarily architectural. Frames now related more to the pictures in them than to the structural style of their surroundings, and here can be seen the beginning of the trend toward simplicity that has lasted into the 20th century.

SOME STYLES. Several dominant styles have remained prominent throughout picture frame history and up to the present. These styles are more versatile than many realize, and they are still being used today to enhance the presentation of art. Some of the most familiar, and the most popular, reproductions of antique mouldings seen are: Spanish Serger 17th century; Italian 17th century; early Dutch; early American; French Louis XIII; French Louis XIV; French Louis XV; and French Louis XVI.

Seventeenth-century Venetian style frame, carved from a solid block of wood. Frame 279 mm x 229 mm (9 in. x 11 in.), moulding 76 mm (3 in.), Aquatint, by Leon Karp. Collection of Mr and Mrs S. Manville

French Louis XIII style frame, gold leaf on gesso. Floral pattern with sand spread within panel area of moulding

Spanish Serger style frame, 17th century, gold leaf on gesso. 330 mm x 356 mm (14 in. x 13 in.)

Frame designed by Hector Guimard, French, 1905-1910. Fruitwood, carved and partly gilt, 486 mm x 584 mm (19⅛ in. x 23 in.). Courtesy of the Cooper-Hewitt Museum of Decorative Arts and Design, Smithsonian Institution, Washington, DC. Gift of Mme Hector Guimard

SOME IMAGINATION. Throughout this book are examples of how pieces can be framed imaginatively. The ones shown here–a family photograph, biscuits made by a child, and a folk art piece– exhibit a warm naturalness in the unconventionality of their presentation. The photograph, object, or picture does not have to be a masterpiece, just something simple and personal. It will assume an added importance when framed with taste and imagination. The essential thing is to live with what you have and not to store it away. What better way to show something off handsomely than to exhibit it in a suitable frame.

Family photograph. An example of imaginative framing for an old photograph. 19th-century frame. Marquetry pattern inlaid with ivory and ebony woods worked into fruitwood frame. Matted with Italian marbelized paper. Photograph 114 mm x 152 mm (4½ in. x 6 in.), frame size 285 mm x 343 mm (11¼ in. x 13½ in.)

"Tugboat" shadow box, *circa* 1890, made from cigar-box wood. An American folk art piece. 254 mm x 356 mm, 50 mm deep (10 in. x 14 in., 2 in. deep). Collection of Herbert W. Hemphill, Jr

"Holiday Cookies," by Lukey. Biscuits and paper cutouts mounted on raised wood panel. Moulding and panel painted. Frame size 279 mm x 229 mm (11 in. x 9 in.). Collection of Mr and Mrs William Sayles

PROTECTION. The well-being of artwork can be affected in many ways. Humidity can cause paper to wrinkle excessively. It can warp paintings done on wooden panels, or photographs that have been mounted on boards. It can cause the flaking of silk-screen inks. Humidity can cause mildew and result in bacterial growths on the art. Extremes of heat or unusual dryness will cause the art to become brittle, and therefore easily destructible. Soot will blacken and stain artwork, and bright light, especially direct sunlight, will fade it.

Each of these conditions and others can reduce the attractiveness of what you plan to frame, as well as its value. A picture frame will contribute significantly to its protection.

PRESENTATION. The second major function of a picture frame is to enhance the presentation of the artwork. It should not detract attention from it. If a frame contrasts excessively with the picture, it is not the appropriate frame, for instead of inconspicuously helping the art, it is hindering it by establishing another very opposite pole to which the viewer must give attention.

If a frame is too narrow for its contents, it will appear insecure, as if it were holding on to the art for dear life, and it will cause the whole presentation to appear flimsy. A frame that is too heavy will smother the art, making it difficult for the viewer to see it. If people who have been to your home can recall that you have something framed on the wall but cannot remember much about what it was, it may well be that the art is not allowed to stand out enough. A picture frame should be properly balanced with the art if it is to perform its aesthetic function of enhancing the presentation of that art. If it is too little or too much, it will detract from the presentation.

When a frame is put around a picture, it does not become a part of that picture–it is simply a pleasing surrounding for it. If it is *not* a pleasing surrounding, then it is the wrong frame for that particular picture. The frame should do for the art what a springtime meadow does for a beautiful maiden.

THIS BOOK. Step-by-step directions are given to help you make a basic frame. They involve measuring and cutting the moulding, joining it to form a frame, applying the backing, and assembling all the components to make the finished frame. Throughout are numerous photographs and diagrams which accompany the text. Each section of the book describes another technique, such as the use of mounts, or liners, or any of the other ways there are of protecting and presenting the art.

At the conclusion of the book is a list of suppliers, and of other books that might interest you.

The basic frame. Glass, picture, and backing ready to be assembled in the frame

Indian rubbing on rice paper. Oak frame, stained and waxed. A white paint wash was applied, then sanded, allowing paint to remain in recessed areas. Mauve-coloured grasscloth mount. Frame 635 mm (25 in.) square, mount 76 mm (3 in.), moulding 19 mm (¾ in.). Collection of Mr and Mrs L. A. Swyer

TYPES OF FRAMING

The examples that appear on these two pages illustrate some of the different framing techniques that are discussed in this book. They represent a varied number of ways that the particular requirements of the art are met by the frame and its components. Not included here, but found elsewhere in the book, are shadow box, glass trap, baguette, mirror framing techniques, and mounting photographs.

Simple framing: glass, picture, and backing. See page 18

Framing with a mount. See page 36

Framing with a fabric mount. See page 40

Framing with a mount, plain or fabric-covered. See page 45

Framing with a liner. See page 46

Framing a canvas. See pages 46 and 63

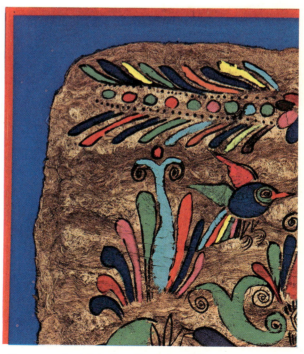

Passe partout framing. See page 74

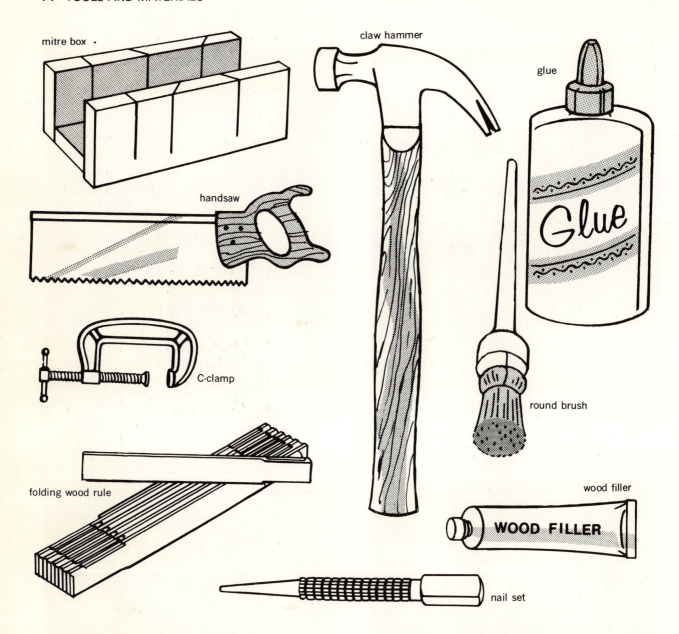

mitre box

claw hammer

glue

handsaw

Glue

C-clamp

round brush

folding wood rule

wood filler

WOOD FILLER

nail set

Tools and Materials

Most of the tools and materials required in picture framing are familiar and easy to use. Some are illustrated here; others are described elsewhere in the book where they apply.

MEASURING AND CUTTING

Mitre box–basic tool for mitring corners of frame. One shown is of simplest variety and requires a jig (page 20) for accurate measuring.

Handsaw–for cutting moulding. Choose one of good quality with 12 teeth to 25 mm (1 in.).

C-clamps–both large and small sizes. Used to hold moulding in position during cutting and joining.

Folding wood rule–best for measuring wood.

JOINING AND NAILING

Claw hammer–choose one that handles comfortably.

Nail set–used to set nails below surface of wood.

Wood filler–for filling nail holes and scratches.

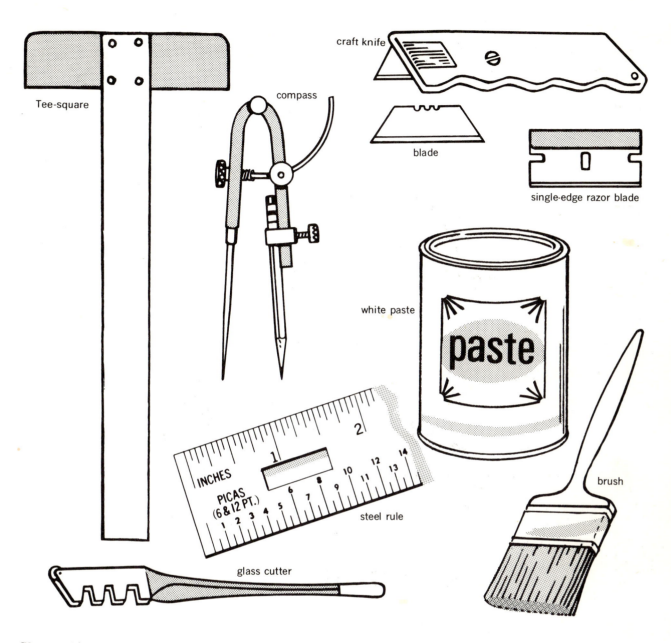

Tee-square

compass

craft knife

blade

single-edge razor blade

white paste

paste

brush

steel rule

INCHES

PICAS (6 & 12 PT.)

glass cutter

Glue–a white resin glue is recommended.

Round brush–for spreading glue on mitred corners.

GLASS CUTTING

Glass cutter–the cutting wheel should be kept in kerosene when not in use.

Steel rule–635 mm (24 in.) long. For accurate measuring of glass, mount and mounting boards.

Tee-square–used as guide for glass cutter and in cutting mounts.

MOULDING

Compass–used to outline the margins of the mount.

Craft knife with replaceable blades–(also called utility knife) for cutting mounts and cardboard. Should be kept sharp.

Single-edge razor blade–can be used to correct rounded corners on mount, plus various other uses.

White paste–for adhering fabric to a mount.

Brush–for spreading paste when covering a mount with fabric.

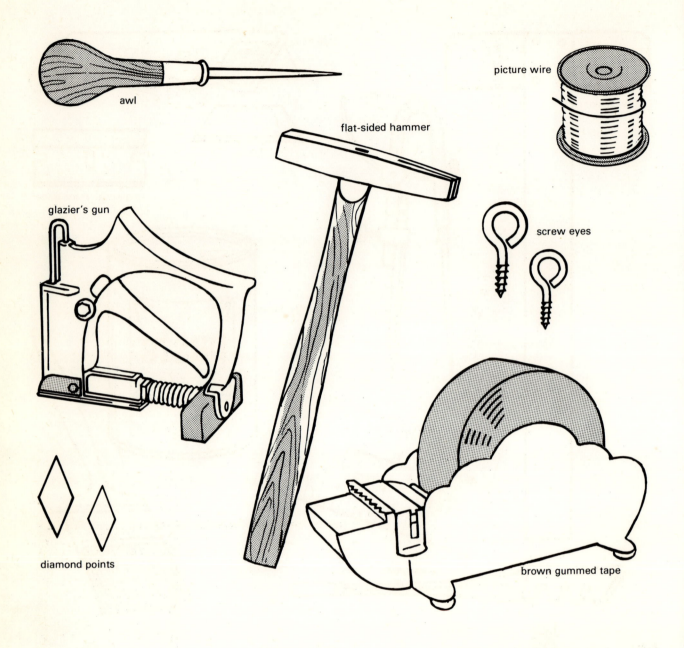

awl

picture wire

flat-sided hammer

glazier's gun

screw eyes

diamond points

brown gummed tape

ASSEMBLY

Awl–used to start shallow holes for brads and screw eyes.

Flat-sided hammer–for driving brads into moulding. Wire cutters may be used instead.

Glazier's gun and diamond points–use in place of brads to contain all the components in the frame.

Brown gummed tape–used in widths of 50 mm or 76 mm (2 in. or 3 in.) depending upon the width of the moulding.

HANGING

Screw eye–small steel loop on a screw. Used to hold the picture wire on the back of the frame.

Picture wire–strung through screw eyes for hanging.

Workshop

The workshop layout shown here is meant to help you plan ahead for the best use of the space you have available. Those who already have a work area can incorporate this plan, or one similar to it, into their present set-up.

It is important to separate the wood-cutting area from the other work areas by either a wall or curtain. This is to avoid sawdust settling on materials and artwork, and also to allow sufficient room when handling long strips of moulding. Uncut moulding should lay flat on shelves to reduce warpage.

There are also separate tables for joining, mount-making, fitting, and finishing, all with adequate storage drawers and shelves for the related tools and materials. The mount-making table can also be used for cutting glass.

The tables should have level tops and be high enough so that you do not have to stoop to work. They should also be sturdy and, if possible, attached to the floor to keep them steady for accurate measuring and cutting.

Neatness is important, as is good lighting and ventilation–the latter particularly where paints and solvents are located.

Key to plan
1 Shelves for mouldings–stored flat
2 Wood-cutting area
3 Joining table
4 Attached vice
5 Fitting table
6 Mount-cutting table
7 Finishing table
8 Waste paper basket

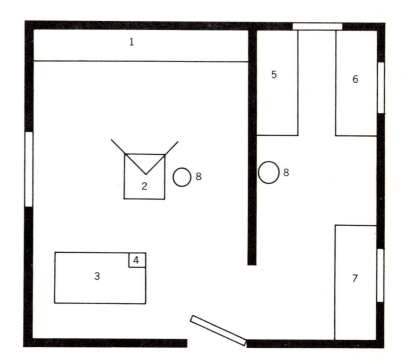

Section of moulding

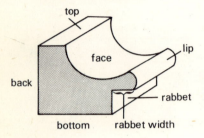

To make a rabbet using wood strip

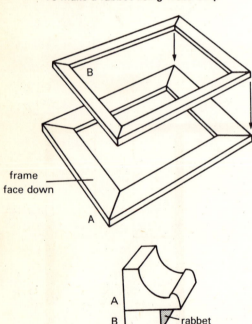

Making a Basic Frame

The step-by-step instructions in this section of the book will enable you to construct a basic frame with professional results. This is the simplest of frames utilizing glass. Every step in its production will be repeated in any frame with glass that you make–with few exceptions. These exceptions occupy the last section of the book.

MOULDINGS. Any wood can be used for the moulding, but some are more popular than others. Basswood, an excellent choice for a beginner, is the most common because it is lightweight, easy to handle, and relatively inexpensive. It is also easily stained or painted. Red oak, in contrast, is heavier, more difficult for a beginner, and more expensive. Its redeeming feature, however, is its outstanding grain. If you can obtain a short length of this wood, do so. Massage a coat of beeswax into it with a clean rag. Buff it with another rag, and see its beauty for yourself. A red oak moulding, 50 mm (2in.) wide, is one of the handsomest grained woods available.

Generally, however, a hardwood picture frame is not as wide as 50 mm (2 in.) since that width moulding in hardwood can dull a saw blade easier than that same width in a softer wood–pine, for example. A narrow hardwood is also easier for a beginner to work with and to drive nails through; wider widths take experience. Walnut is rarely made into a frame wider than 19 mm (¾ in.). It does not require anything other than a wax finish, for this wood is especially valued for its beautiful grain and colour. Pine is usually not kiln-dried and will sometimes leak resin. This can be remedied by sealing the moulding with a coat of shellac after it has been cut and joined into a frame.

SELECTION. Picture-frame mouldings can be obtained from picture-frame shops or from timber suppliers. Frames can also be made from builder's mouldings such as those used as trim for windows and doors. The timber supplier will usually have a wider selection of these than of picture-frame mouldings, and the cost will be less per running foot. Since these mouldings are used for building purposes, they will not have a rabbet. (The rabbet, which is required to hold the picture in place, is the groove under the lip of the moulding–see diagram.) Such a moulding, however, is easily adapted for picture frames by attaching a strip of wood to its underside.

The strip should be at least 6 mm (¼ in.) wide and 10 mm (⅜ in.) deep, and can be either glued or nailed in place. (If nailed, be careful not to cut into the nails when sawing the moulding.) You can also make two rectangles, one with a wider window opening than the other (see diagram), and when the second shape is attached to the first one, a rabbet will be formed automatically.

If the moulding is sufficiently thick, the timberyard will cut a rabbet directly into it for you, or if you have a power saw (such as a table or radial saw with a rip blade), you can do it yourself. Most rabbets do not require more than a 6 mm (¼ in.) width, so the blade should be kept very low throughout the operation. Canvases may require a deeper rabbet.

To find out how long a length of moulding to buy for a frame, add together the 4 sides of the picture, plus 8 times the width of the moulding you have chosen, plus a cutting allowance of 50 mm (2 in.). For a 203 mm x 254 mm (8 in. x 10 in.) picture, using a moulding 50 mm (2 in.) wide, you would add 203 mm + 203 mm + 254 mm + 254 mm + 406 mm + 50 mm (8 in. + 8 in. + 10 in. + 10 in. + 16 in. + 2 in.) for a total 1,372 mm (54 in.) of moulding length.

measuring

There are two ways of measuring for a frame. Generally the *rabbet size* is the measurement used when a picture is being framed without a mount, as here. *Frame sight size* is usually the measure when a specific area is to be shown, or when a mount is being used and will be cut to fit a particular frame (see page 36). *Frame sight size* refers to what will be visible from the front of the frame. *Rabbet size* refers to the larger opening at the back of the frame.

The rabbet size will always be *larger* than the frame sight size by *twice* the width of the rabbet. This is so that the components (picture, glass, backing, etc) can be accommodated comfortably. Conversely, the frame sight size will always be *smaller* than the rabbet size by twice the width of the rabbet. This insures that the components will be held securely in place by the lip of the frame which overlaps them.

When you are using rabbet size as your measurement, you must be sure to make the rabbet-size dimensions slightly larger than the dimensions of the picture you are framing. A 2 mm ($\frac{1}{16}$ in.) tolerance on each side is usually sufficient. This is so that you will be able to slide the picture into the frame easily. Assuming that the picture is 203 mm x 254 mm (8 in. x 10 in.), a tolerance of 3 mm (⅛ in.) added to the picture dimensions would give you a rabbet size of 206 mm x 257 mm (8⅛ in. x 10⅛ in.). If the width of the rabbet on each side is 6 mm (¼ in.), the opening at the front of the frame would then be 12 mm (½ in.) less (twice the width of the rabbet) than the rabbet size, making a frame sight size of 194 mm x 244 mm (7⅝ in. x 9⅝ in.). If the rabbet size is your measurement, mark the dimensions on the rabbet of the moulding; for frame sight size, mark on the lip of the moulding.

A folding rule is best for measuring wood, and a steel tape rule for art, mounts, and cardboard backing. A good method of measuring accurately is to begin at the 25 mm (1 in.) mark, using it as zero. When using this method *remember* to subtract 25 mm (1 in.) from the final measurements in order to obtain the true dimensions.

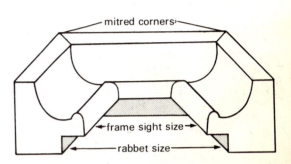

Cross-section of frame

mitred corners

frame sight size

rabbet size

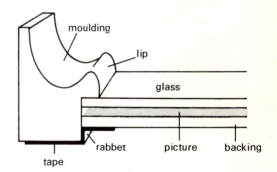

Profile of assembled frame

moulding

lip

glass

rabbet   picture   backing

tape

Mitre Cutting

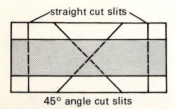

Mitre box

straight cut slits

45° angle cut slits

Once the dimensions for the frame have been determined, the moulding is measured and the sides are cut at 45° angles. Accuracy in cutting these angles, or mitres, is essential for a perfect join at the corners. The basic tools are a mitre box and handsaw. For the beginner the simplest mitre box is probably best, but if you plan to make a number of frames, it will be more economical to buy one which will last longer and be more efficient.

mitre box

A jig, or stop-block, is helpful for obtaining accurate moulding lengths. It is made by mitring a yardstick at one end and nailing it to the bottom inside of mitre box, aligning the mitre with the first slit. Then mitre a block of wood on one side and clamp it to the yardstick at the moulding distance to be registered (see diagram).

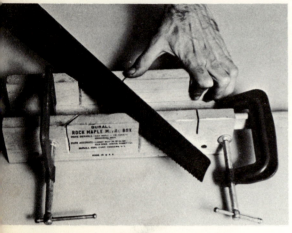

To hold moulding stationary for cutting, secure to mitre box with C-clamps

It is important that the moulding remain in a stationary position for cutting. This can be done with C-clamps, as shown. Avoid placing clamps on the moulding face, but if you cannot, put a cushioning of wood or cardboard between them. Try to use the rabbet as a grip–but not its lip, since this is the weakest part of the moulding.

The mitre box should be checked at intervals for accuracy since saw cuts can chip and widen the slits. To do this, put a piece of firm cardboard in the channel, then insert a ruler or Tee-square in the slit as a guide. Press guide to slit and draw a line on the cardboard against it. Check the angle with a protractor; if not accurate, you should get a new mitre box. Also check the saw blade–it should be very sharp. If it isn't, the cut will be rough, making a clean join difficult. Also, a dull blade tends to drag the moulding rather than cut cleanly through, resulting in an inaccurate angle.

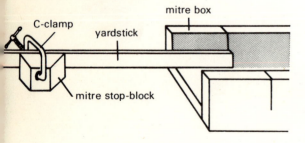

Mitre jig assembly

C-clamp

yardstick

mitre box

mitre stop-block

table saw and radial saw

These saws usually come with a mitre gauge. However, you can make your own–if you don't have one, or if it is broken, or if you find it is too troublesome to readjust for the mitres.

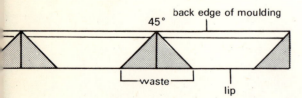

45°

back edge of moulding

waste

lip

Mitred edges. Cut two longer lengths first, then the shorter ones

BASIC MITRE GAUGE. Cut a 12 mm (½ in.) thick board (fibreboard, Masonite or plywood) to cover the cutting area. Also mitre two strips of wood at one end, 25 mm x 50 mm (1 in. x 2 in.) are fine. Square off the board by determining its centre and drawing a square around it. Draw diagonal lines from each corner and glue the 25 mm x 50 mm (1 in. x 2 in.) along these lines, mitred ends meeting tightly at the vertex of the angle formed by the diagonals, as shown. Measure wood strips to fit into the troughs of table saw (or base of radial saw) and glue them to the bottom of the board. Cut through the mitre and just enough through the board to make passage for table saw. For radial saw, cut through the mitre and make a slight groove in the board.

A saw blade guard (see diagram) will help you control the pushing and pulling of the mitre. Glue two pieces of 102 mm (4 in.) wide Masonite to insides of 25 mm x 50 mm (1 in. x 2 in.) and then glue a triangular piece over them. Screw in a small handle.

cutting the moulding

For accurate angles when using a mitre box, hold saw vertical to the cut that is to be made. When using the basic mitre gauge with a table saw, place the rabbet side against one 25 mm x 50 mm (1 in. x 2 in.). Hold moulding firmly with one hand and guard handle with the other. Push gauge to cut the moulding. Return gauge until saw blade disappears under the guard. For radial saw, push gauge away while simultaneously pressing it firmly against the base of the saw. CAUTION: don't let go of gauge or moulding while blade is exposed. When bracing the moulding against the 25 mm x 50 mm (1 in. x 2 in.), don't hold it where the cut will be made.

First cut one end of the moulding in order to have a mitred edge with which to start. A good habit to get into is to cut long sides first, so that if a mistake is made, the pieces can still be used for the short sides. To measure rabbet size for a 203 mm x 254 mm (8 in. x 10 in.) picture and a 6 mm (¼ in.) rabbet width, mark off 257 mm (10⅛ in.) on the rabbet. Make a pencil dot at the bottom of rabbet so that when moulding is put into the channel there will be no space between the mark and the slit. This is so you can see exactly where to cut. On table or radial saw, there should be no space between the mark and the gauge. (If frame sight size is your measure, mark off 244 mm (9⅝ in.) on the lip of the moulding.)

Cut the moulding where marked. Repeat for the second long side. For a mitre box, change slits. For table or radial saw, place moulding on the opposite gauge, as shown. Before cutting the short sides, mitre one end of the moulding just as you did for the long sides.

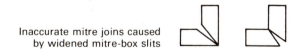
Inaccurate mitre joins caused by widened mitre-box slits

When all four sides are cut, remove rough wood fibres on ends with sandpaper. Don't actually sand the wood, just tap it to get rid of any particles that may interfere with joining. Brush moulding free of sawdust, expecially at ends. Place the four pieces on a flat surface, equal sides opposite and fronts facing–ready to be joined.

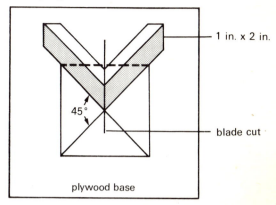
Mitre gauge for table saw
1 in. x 2 in.
45°
blade cut
plywood base

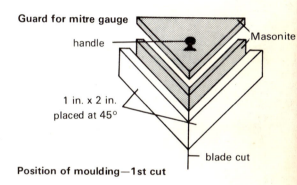
Guard for mitre gauge
handle
Masonite
1 in. x 2 in. placed at 45°
blade cut

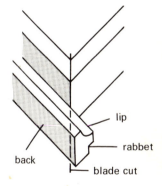
Position of moulding—1st cut
lip
rabbet
back
blade cut

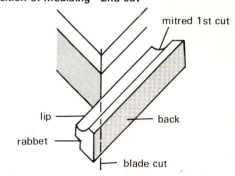
Position of moulding—2nd cut
mitred 1st cut
lip
back
rabbet
blade cut

Joining

A white resin glue is best for joining wood, and Uhu's glue is probably the most popular. Also needed are alligator clips, obtainable in hardware and electrical supply stores, or corner cramps. Upon purchase, file their teeth a little sharper with a triangular file.

Apply glue to all mitred ends in quick succession. By the time you finish the last end, the first will be sufficiently tacky for joining. Bring all sides together and adjust until they meet properly. Attach alligator clips to the corners to hold them in place.

If the frame is out of square, springs are used to square it off. Springs are actually upholstery springs cut and shaped to grip the corners of the frame (see diagram at bottom of page 23). Use the springs' tension to grip two sides of the frame at each corner that has a short diagonal. Measure the diagonals again. If the springs have made the short diagonal longer than the long diagonal, there is too much pressure. To reduce it, remove the springs and grip them closer to the corners. Measure again and continue to adjust until both diagonals are equal. Don't rush; be patient in order to do a good job. It is very important to have the frame squared. When both diagonals measure equal, allow the frame to dry for several hours. If the weather is rainy, allow to dry for one day. During the first half-hour of drying, do not subject the frame or the surface it is on to any vibration. Check squareness when dry.

1 Setup for joining: four moulding strips, brush, glue, and alligator clips

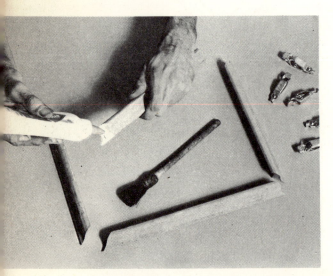

2 Apply light but thorough coat of wood glue to mitred ends. Cover completely

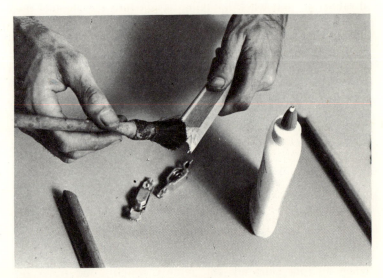

3 Spread glue on ends with brush. Keep equal sides opposite as they are replaced on table

4 Bring a long and short side together and adjust until they meet for perfect join

5 Repeat for opposite sides. Apply alligator clips to outside corners

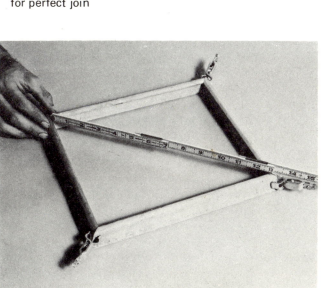

6 Clips should grip wood so as to exert pressure towards corners. Check for squareness by measuring diagonals with a wood rule

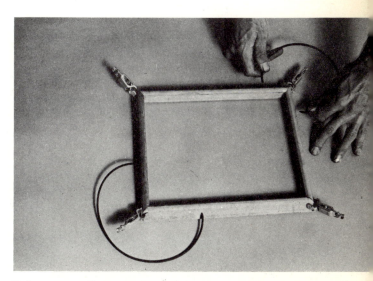

7 Squaring off the frame: Springs make short diagonal longer and long one shorter. Keep on until glued ends have dried

Upholstery spring cut and bent to shape

Nailing

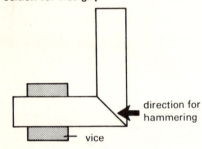

Direction nails enter mitred corners

Position for vice grip

direction for hammering

vice

If they are to remain joined, the mitre corners must be secured with nails. Each corner in turn is held in a vice, and nails are driven directly into the moulding. However, if you have an electric drill you will be able to make holes for the nails first. Just brace the drill into a vice parallel to the floor and lock the trigger in the "on" position.

The nail holes should not be as wide as the nails, nor should they be as deep. Consider the width of the moulding in order to determine the depth of the nail holes. For example, if the moulding is 50 mm (2 in.) wide, and you plan to use 50 mm (2 in.) nails, a hole of the same depth would diminish the effectiveness of the nail. In this case a 25 mm (1 in.) hole would be preferable. Drill the holes through one side of the moulding and slightly into the other. If the drill bit comes through the surface anywhere, do not try to correct it, for you might make an even wider hole. Just drill a new hole.

Two nails are sufficient for most corners. For narrow mouldings use two brads. If a moulding is wide, cross the nails, putting two

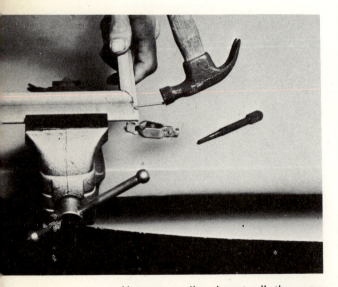

Hammer nails almost all the way. The frame side being hammered is gripped in vice to absorb shock

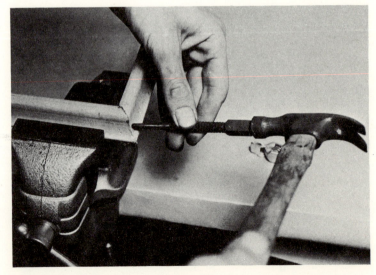

Sink nails just below surface with nail set. Repeat nailing and countersinking for other corners

in one side of a corner and one in the other (see diagram). Some very wide or high mouldings may require four nails. Often nails of two or more sizes are used for one moulding. You can, for example, use nails in combination with brads.

Do all four corners, sinking each nail below the surface with a nail set. Then fill in nail holes with wood filler. Use a colour close to that of the wood in order to avoid conspicuously coloured dots at each corner. Also fill any dents or misdirected holes or any scratches made by the alligator clips during joining.

The entire frame is then sanded lightly with fine sandpaper, with special attention given to the corners. The joints should be so smooth that you can't feel them with your fingers. Keep in mind that any imperfections will be emphasized by the finish that is to be applied. Remove all sawdust with a cloth and use a soft brush to get into the corners. Insure that the frame is absolutely clean before proceeding further.

Note that at this point the frame has been made. All that remains is to put a finish on it.

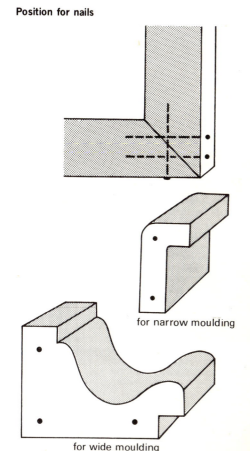

Position for nails

for narrow moulding

for wide moulding

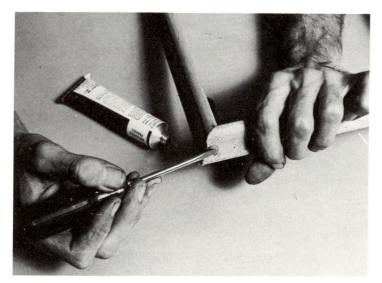

Fill nail holes and any scratches with wood filler. Then allow to dry

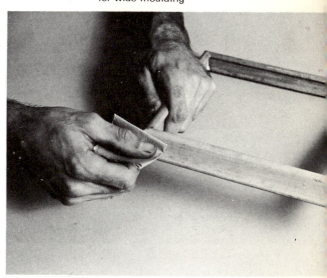

Sand entire frame with medium then fine sandpaper until smooth. Pay special attention to the corners

Applying a wax finish. Be sure the wood is well sanded before the wax is rubbed in

Applying a stain finish. Staining brings out the grain of the wood

Toning. Black and raw umber pigments are mixed with the stain for varied effects

Finishes

When considering the finish for a frame, keep in mind that the frame serves a dual purpose. Mainly it is to protect the artwork, but it is also to enhance that art by relating to it in a way that complements both the subject and its surroundings, and it should do this unobtrusively.

There are a number of different finishes, but basically they are of two types: those that treat the surface of the wood to emphasize its grain, such as wax and stain; and those that are meant to decorate, such as paint and metal leaf. Before applying any finish, make certain that the wood is thoroughly sanded and free of dust. While applying, allow every coat to dry properly before proceeding further.

WAXED SURFACES Most mouldings with an interesting grain need nothing more than this type of treatment. The use of a paste wax, such as Beeswax, deepens the tone of the wood slightly and creates a more pronounced grain pattern. This finish is frequently seen on walnut and oak frames. If the frame is pine or some other wood that has not been kiln-dried, you will have to seal it first with a light coat of shellac thinned with wood alcohol.

The waxing process is simple. With a cloth, coat the wood generously with wax and work it in well. Wipe off the excess and buff vigorously. The frame should now have a very soft, subtle sheen. If you wish an even smoother surface and one with a slight glaze, rub the wood down with steel wool after sanding. Then wipe the frame thoroughly to remove all traces of steel dust and burrs. Wax as before and buff.

STAINED SURFACES Another type of clean, attractive finish can be given to wood by applying a liquid stain, usually available in many different shades.

To apply, wet a soft cloth with the stain and then work it into the wood. You can mix different shades of stain for the desired result and can tone them down with powdered pigments such as black and raw umber. The effects of toning can be most clearly seen when used on light-coloured woods such as basswood and pine. Experiment for possible variations on some wood scraps, using a stain and black and raw umber pigments. After the frame has been stained, buff it with a cloth until it has a very soft sheen. If you prefer a more brilliant finish, rub with fine steel wool, dust off well, and rebuff.

A natural stain can also be used. Its light tone permits a wide range of variations. Stain as before, then mix one part orange shellac to four parts denatured alcohol. Add a small amount of raw umber or rottenstone (a grey dustlike powder) to tone down the shellac colour. Dip a toothbrush, or any stiff brush, into the mixture and scrape your finger across it to "splatter" the frame. This will deepen the tone of the finish. You can add more raw umber, or even black pigment, to achieve other tones. Buff when finished.

You can build upon this surface by adding "flyspecks." Make a puddle of the shellac mixture on the table surface and add small amounts of raw umber and black pigments. Mix with a brush and test on scrap wood or cardboard. You should have very tiny dark dots. It may be necessary to spread this mixture around for a while in order to get the speckled effect you want. When you think you have it, apply a *thin* coat to the frame and then buff. The finish can now be softened by brushing on some rottenstone. Work it with a dry brush, then wipe off the excess.

PAINTED SURFACES A plastic paint, such as Artex, should be used. The first coat should be light, but thoroughly applied. If the wood is deeply grained, you may have to work the paint into it with the brush. You can thin the paint with water for this purpose. When the first coat is completely dry (about half an hour), apply a second coat. Apply a third coat if you feel the frame requires it. Use steel wool and buff with a rag after second and third coats. For a very smooth surface, use thicker coats of paint after the first coat. You may have to apply two or three. Rub with steel wool after each one.

Gesso, which is a powdered chalk similar to plaster of Paris, will give a surface approaching the smoothness of marble. Apply several coats, allowing each one to dry about fifteen minutes. When the last coat has been applied, allow about three hours for a complete drying, then sand the surface smooth with silver sandpaper. Be patient, for the surface will be rough. Inspect the frame from several angles for any leftover rough spots, particularly in the corners and depressions of the frame.

When the surface is smooth to the touch, as well as to the eye, apply a coat of paint. Then steel wool lightly and apply a second coat. Repeat for a third coat. This will probably be sufficient, but

Corner detail of Florentine style frame. An example of a new frame stressed to look aged. The design was scratched out of gessoed surface. Gold leaf was put onto design and moulding trim. Then red paint was applied to panel section, toning it. Frame was then antiqued

if you want to eliminate any tiny flaws and assure an even surface, apply a coat of spray paint. Steel wool lightly again. The surface should now be very smooth, with no grain pattern in evidence.

GILDED SURFACES. Metal leafing is a substitute for the traditional gold-leafing process which is more expensive and more difficult to do, generally requiring years of experience. Metal leaf comes in two colours: gold (actually bronze) and silver (actually aluminium). Before gilding, the wood is coated with brownish-red paint, which is intended to imitate the red clay size used under real gold-leafing. When dry, rub smooth with steel wool, then seal the surface with two coats of shellac and allow to dry. Apply a thin coat of gold size. This will take about two hours to get tacky-and that is when the metal leaf should be put on.

Metal leaf comes in sheets, 25 to a book and each approximately 127 mm (5 in.) square. For narrow mouldings, cut book to size. To lift a leaf from the book, pass a soft brush over your skin to pick up any grease (or use Vaseline) and then touch it to one edge of the leaf. The leaf should cling to the brush. Lay leaf on the moulding and tamp down gently. When the entire surface is leafed, tamp down in any places where the leaf did not completely adhere.

Permit the frame to dry for at least eight hours, then brush off any excess leaf, rub the entire surface with a soft cloth, and apply a light coat of shellac. If you wish, you can now tone the frame with splatter, flyspecks, or rottenstone as described in Stained Surfaces.

If you want to gild just part of the frame and paint another part, first apply shellac where the leafing will be and then paint the rest of the frame. Gesso can also be used for gilding. It makes a smoother surface and obscures any wood grain.

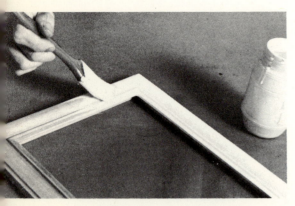

1 Preparing the wood for metal leafing. Gesso is applied for smoother surface, allowed to dry, and then rubbed down with sandpaper

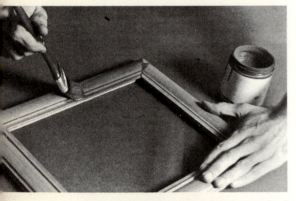

2 Brownish-red paint (undercoating) is brushed onto surface and rubbed with steel wool when dry

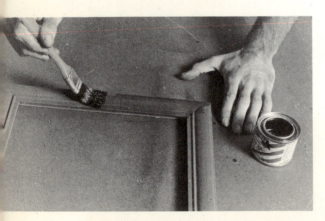

3 Wood is shellacked, and thin coat of gold size is brushed on. Metal leaf adheres where size is applied

4 Leaves are overlapped and then tamped down onto the moulding, gently, with a brush. Trim excess

Glass Cutting

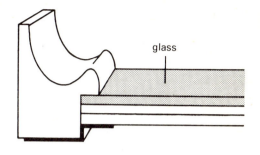

Glass is generally required for surfaces which need protection, such as watercolours, pastels, gouaches, and prints. It also adds depth, and gives, to the picture or photograph, an importance it might not otherwise seem to have. Picture glass, or 16-oz glass, is thinner and clearer than window glass. Be sure to inspect it for flaws. Non-glare glass, also available, is more expensive and, because of its slight opacity, tends to dim light colours and delicate lines. Usually the glazier you buy glass from will cut it to size, but you can do it yourself and save money. It is not difficult, and once you try you will realize how quickly it can be mastered.

Keep the glass clean and free of dust. Work on a firm surface such as a cardboard-covered table. If the cardboard has to be levelled, pad newspapers or an old rug under it. When cutting, keep these points in mind: 1. Begin at the edge farthest from you and cut straight towards you to the near edge, applying a constant pressure. You don't have to go fast. 2. *Do not repeat a cut.* This ruins the wheel of your cutter and might break the glass.

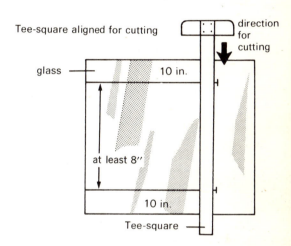

You will need a glass cutter, a Tee-square, a ruler, and a soft lead pencil. The cutter, available in hardware stores, should be stored with its wheel in kerosene to keep it rust-free and insure a clean cut. For a 203 mm x 254 mm (8 in. x 10 in.) glass, measure the 254 mm (10 in.) sides as shown at the right. Turn the glass so that the cut will be perpendicular to you. Once the measure is marked with the pencil, place the cutter on the far mark and slide the Tee-square up to it. By moving the cutter you will see a small space between the mark and the Tee-square. Adjust the Tee-square until it is that same space from the second mark. Do this by sight, then check with the cutter. It should touch the Tee-square. Return cutter to the first mark and check that the Tee-square has not moved. Adjust and check until both points are the same distance from the Tee-square. When this is done, cut the glass as shown in photo at right. The result will be a glass 254 mm (10 in.) wide. Repeat for the 203 mm (8 in.) sides.

For those with a good eye and steady hand, or sufficient experience in cutting glass, there is an alternative method which saves time. The only tool is the cutter. The frame is placed face down on the work surface, and the glass is placed over it—one straight edge of the glass aligned with the corners of the rabbet. After the glass has been cut (as shown at the bottom of page 30), the glass should fit into the rabbet a little loosely. Stand the frame on one edge, and holding the glass in it, look through to the front. If an edge of glass is visible, it was cut too short. If no edge is visible, and you did not have to force the glass flat against the frame it is a perfect fit.

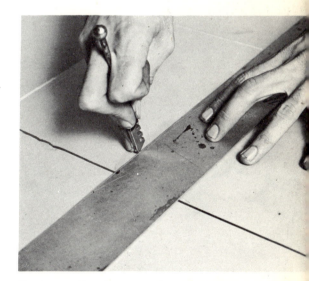

Cut long sides first. Press down on Tee-square. Start at edge farthest from you, cut towards you and *over* nearest edge. Result should be a straight cut

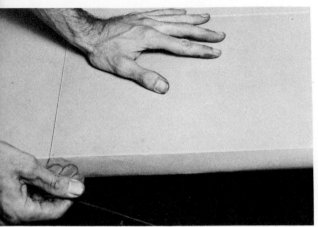

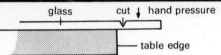

glass | cut ↓ hand pressure

table edge

Align cut a bit beyond table edge. Grip excess glass and snap off with downward pressure. Measure as before and cut the shorter sides

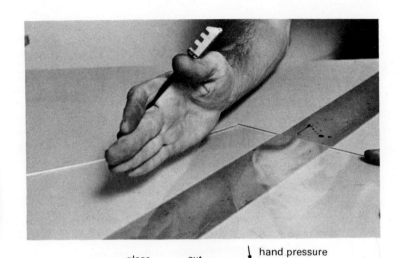

glass | cut | ↓ hand pressure

Tee-square

Or snap glass by sliding Tee-square under, aligned with cut. Press down on excess or chop sharply with side of hand

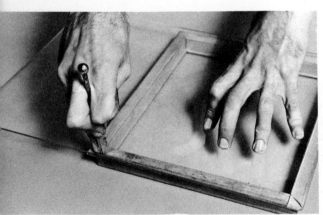

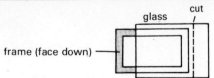

glass | cut

frame (face down)

1 Sight cutting. Frame face down. Using opposite rabbet as guide, cut just inside frame edge. Move glass a bit over edge and snap off excess

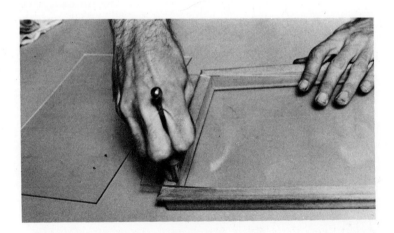

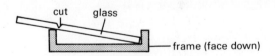

cut | glass

frame (face down)

2 Slide glass into rabbet. Fit should not be tight. Cut opposite sides. Since glass rests at angle, cut about 2 mm ($\frac{1}{16}$ in.) in from frame edge

Backing

The backing board, which acts as a support for the picture and the glass, is the last element of the basic picture frame. Corrugated board or double-thick chipboard, available in art-supply stores, are most commonly used for backing.

Of the two, chipboard is firmer, smoother, and usually flatter. It is also more expensive and much heavier. Its weight is an important consideration when a large frame is being made, especially if that frame will have glass-which adds weight-or if it has a narrow moulding.

Corrugated board usually has one slightly bowed side. This can be an advantage during fitting, for if the board is placed curved side down in the frame, it will increase pressure against the glass and thus help to keep everything in the frame pressed flat. Its one disadvantage is the ribbing which, after a period of years, can impress its pattern upon the art.

Mark and cut the backing board as shown in the photographs below.

The backing board can also be cut to the same size as the picture, or slightly larger-by about 2 mm ($\frac{1}{16}$ in.) on each side-but not so large that it will fit tightly when placed in the rabbet.

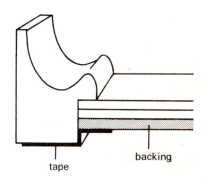

tape   backing

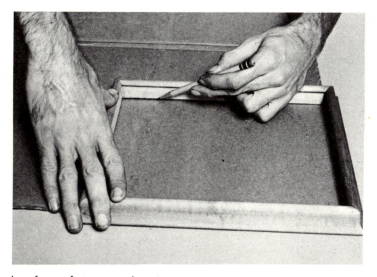

Lay frame face up and at one corner of backing board. Using the rabbet as guide, mark board for cutting

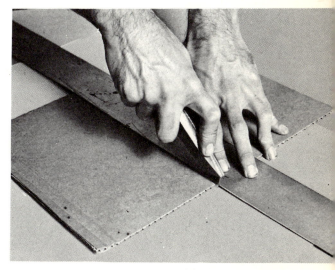

Cut on inside edge of marks. Board should be slightly smaller than rabbet

Assembly

In this important part of frame-making, the components will be fitted into the finished frame and secured. The biggest problem to be encountered is dust. If you are not careful, you will fit the frame and hang it only to see tiny specks between the picture and the glass. Poor workmanship at this point can also result in everything in the frame eventually loosening. Patience now will justify all the care taken up to this point and will result in a well-assembled picture.

PREPARATION. Work on a flat, clean area with enough room to move the frame around. First wet a rag with a cleaning solution— a good one is two parts water to one part denatured alcohol–and wash both sides of the glass and the edges, then wipe thoroughly with a dry rag. If the solution is allowed to dry by itself, it will probably streak. Commercial window cleaners leave a film and should be avoided.

Remove any dust on picture and backing with a soft brush. Put the backing board down, place the picture on it, and then the glass. If you are using corrugated board, lay it curved side up. Check that no dirt has entered between picture and glass. Place the frame face down, pick up the components as one piece, turn them over, and lower them into the frame. Stand the frame up and inspect it from the front to see if everything is in place. This is a final check to spot dirt or fingermarks. Once you are satisfied, return the frame to its face down position.

To secure the components in the frame, drive brads into the moulding at 102 mm (4 in.) intervals, or use a glazier's gun and diamond points. These can be obtained at most hardware stores.

Picture, glass, and backing ready to be assembled in frame

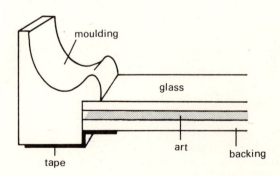

TAPING. Brown gummed paper tape is used to seal the frame against dirt. It should be wide enough to cover the brads or diamond points and still touch the moulding and backing. A 50 mm (2 in.) tape is sufficient for a narrow moulding, but could be too thin for a wide one. In that case, a 76 mm (3 in.) tape is preferable. Its thickness increases its strength, so that it is not as easy to puncture and is better able to withstand the changes in atmosphere that, in time, cause weaker tapes to buckle and peel.

Start taping at any side. Cut the tape a little larger than the side to be taped, wet it, and lay it flat on the bottom of the moulding, about 2 mm ($\frac{1}{16}$ in.) in from the outer edge. Press it onto the wood. With a single-edge razor blade slit the tape up to the corners of the rabbet and continue the slit right across the bottom of the moulding, cutting off the tape at either end. Working from the centre outwards to avoid wrinkling the tape, press it down firmly along the bottom of the moulding, into the rabbet wall, and onto the backing board. Repeat for the opposite side of the frame. See photographs on page 34.

For the two other sides, apply the tape as before, but slit it just up to the corners of the rabbet. Press the tape down as before and trim off the overhang on both sides. Be sure to cut short of these sides so that no tape will be seen from the front of the frame.

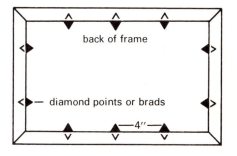

back of frame

diamond points or brads

—4″—

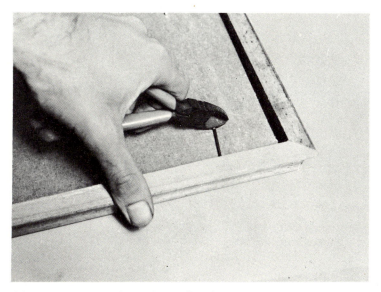

After components have been fitted into frame, place 12 mm (½ in.) brads flat against backing board at 100 mm (4 in.) intervals. Press in with wire cutters

Or use glazier's gun with diamond points. To absorb force, press a brace against the frame when points are shot in

1 Tape is put onto backing to seal frame against dirt. Lay tape 2 mm ($\frac{1}{16}$ in.) in from outer edge. Press into wood and onto backing

2 Slit tape to corners of rabbet and across bottom of moulding. This is done for two opposite sides. Note finished result below

3 For the other sides, tape is slit just to corners of rabbet, and overhang is trimmed off

Details of finished corner. Note how tape is pressed firmly against bottom of moulding

Hanging the Picture

Hanging picture frames is easier than many realize. To avoid undue stress on the moulding, secure the supports, usually screw eyes, to the heaviest component of the frame. For example, if a strainer is used (page 72), it will probably be heavier than the frame, and it is into this that the supports should be anchored. If a baguette has been nailed around a canvas (page 66), fix supports into the canvas stretcher, since that is heavier than the baguette strip.

WIRING. Screw eyes and picture wire can be obtained in any hardware store. Just be sure that the screw eyes are the right size: small ones for narrow mouldings and larger ones for wide mouldings.

To determine the placement of the screw eyes, measure one-third down from the top of the frame. For example, if the frame is 406 mm x 508 mm (16 in. x 20 in.) and is to hang vertically, measure about 165 mm (6½ in.) down, 127 mm (5 in.) if it is going to hang horizontally. Use an awl or brad to start shallow holes for screw eyes. With pliers or wire cutters, screw the eyes into the wood. If there is any danger that they will penetrate through to the other side, they are too long for the moulding.

If you attach the wire as follows, it will not slip out of the screw eyes: Cut wire about 203 mm (8 in.) longer than horizontal side of frame. Slip one end through screw eye, pull it out to about 100 mm (4 in.), slip it through again, and twist short end tightly around main wire. Slip opposite end through the other screw eye. Pull it slightly to leave a little slack, then slip it through screw eye and twist the end around the main wire. Test grip of screw eyes. If loose, re-do them with new holes. Tug wire several times. It should feel secure.

Very large or heavy frames, or those whose dimensions exceed 508 mm x 610 mm (20 in. x 24 in.) need four screw eyes as a precaution against one being pulled out of its hole. Locate the two extra screw eyes about a third of the way up from the bottom of the frame. The wire is attached through them and is simply slipped through the two upper ones (see diagram on page 73). There is additional hardware available for hanging unusually large frames or mirrors; their choice depends upon what is to be supported.

HANGING. The safest support for a frame is a picture hook. If the frame is sufficiently lightweight, just nail the hook directly into the plaster. A double picture hook will take more weight. As an extra precaution, to protect the wall, criss-cross two short pieces of tape over the point where you intend to drive the picture hook. This will help restrict the area that will be weakened by the puncture. If the frame is heavy, you should use a rawlplug set (taking your instructions from the box).

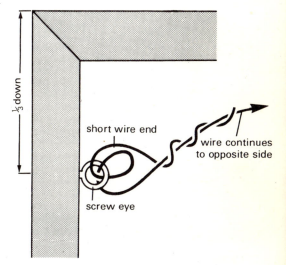

Method of wiring. Slip wire through screw eye, pull out to about 100 mm (4 in.) and slip through again. Twist short end tightly around longer one.

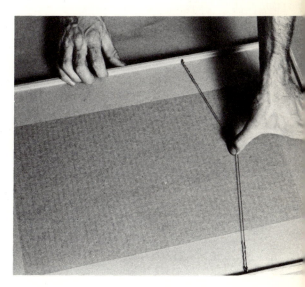

Completed wiring for frame. Note that the wire should have some slack to it

Mounts

A mount is a cardboard with a window cut in it through which the picture is seen. It serves to separate the picture from the frame and its surroundings, and, like the frame, it should relate to the art and enhance its presentation. Its aesthetic role has increased as the frame itself has become simpler, but its practical purpose remains—to prevent the medium from coming into contact with the glass and adhering to it. This is a common concern with watercolours, prints, and, most particularly, pastels.

The main considerations in selecting a mount are proportion, colour, and texture in relation to both picture and frame. Any excessiveness, especially in proportion, will serve to detract from the picture.

There is no rule as to standard widths; let your eye be your guide. Generally, however, the smaller the art, the larger the mount, and vice versa. A mount too narrow for its setting will appear unnecessary, and one too wide will monopolize attention. Avoid a repetition of widths—that is, try not to use a mount of the same or almost the same width as the frame or the art. If all three widths are varied harmoniously no single one will seem out of place. The variety of possibilities is great; experiment to find those that are neither dull nor obtrusive. A good selection of colours and textures is available from which to choose a mount that complements the art and relates to its surroundings.

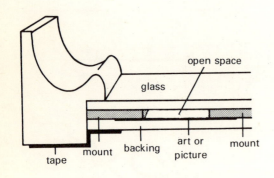

1 Measure width and height of picture to be mounted

2 With mountboard and frame both face up, mark outside size of mount. Cut just short of marks, making mount 3 mm (⅛ in.) smaller than rabbet size.
The mount extends from rabbet to window

MOUNT BOARD. The most common are grey chipboard, regular mountboard, and 100 per cent fibreboard, available at art supply stores. Chipboard, the least expensive and the lowest in quality, is used for mounts that will be covered with fabric. Regular mountboard is the one most often used. Fibreboard is of the highest quality and should be used for art that is especially valuable. The difference between mountboard and fibreboard is acidity. Mountboard contains wood-pulp acids which, over a period of years, discolour paper and contribute to its degeneration. Fibreboard is chemically neutral and does not affect the art adversely.

MEASURING. Once mount dimensions are determined, those for the frame can be determined and the frame made. Measure the art; then establish mount border width. The mount border will overlap the art all around. To find mount sight size (window dimensions), subtract this overlap from the art dimensions. To find frame sight size, add the mount border to each dimension. To find rabbet size, measure rabbet width and add to each dimension.

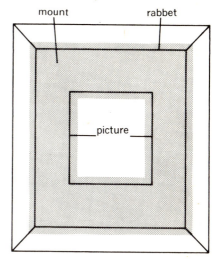

The mount extends from rabbet to window

For example

406 mm x 508 mm (16 in. x 20 in.)	406 mm	(16 in.)	508 mm	(20 in.)	
3 mm + 3 mm (⅛ in. + ⅛ in.)	− 6 mm	(¼ in.)	− 6 mm	(¼ in.)	
	400 mm	(15¾ in.)	502 mm	(19¾ in.)	(mount sight size)
76 mm + 76 mm (3 in. + 3 in.)	+152 mm	(21¾ in.)	+152 mm	(21¾ in.)	
	552 mm	(21¾ in.)	654 mm	(25¾ in.)	(frame sight size)
6 mm + 6 mm (¼ in. + ¼ in.)	+ 12 mm	(½ in.)	+ 12 mm	(½ in.)	
	564 mm	(22¼ in.)	666 mm	(26¼ in.)	(rabbet size)

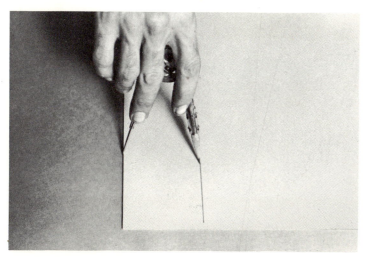

3 Turn mount face down. See directions for measuring mount border width on page 39. Start at far end and draw compass towards you

4 Back of mountboard now has margins all around, marking window area to be cut out. Note that lines are drawn to edges

An example of a gouache painting mounted with white board with a basswood moulding. The moulding was finished with two different coloured stains. Frame size 584 mm x 483 mm (23 in. x 19 in.), mount 127 mm (5 in.) top and sides, 133 mm (5¼ in.) bottom

If you are taking rabbet size as the measurement for the frame, measure and mark dimensions on the rabbet of the moulding. If you are taking frame sight size, measure and mark on the lip of the moulding.

Sometimes the bottom of the mat is made wider than the top and sides to compensate for an optical illusion which causes it to appear narrower. The additional width is usually 12 mm (½ in.). This would add 165 mm (6½ in.) to the 400 mm (15¾ in.) mount sight size if the picture is to hang horizontally, but if it is to hang vertically add the 165 mm (6½ in.) to the 500 mm (19¾ in.) measure.

If you have a print with the artist's signature or the print number, or both, and you want them revealed, just cut a large enough window. If the window overlap covers more than you desire, or if you want the edges of the paper to show, consider a mount. See page 45.

The outside dimensions of the mount are obtained by measuring a rectangle 3 mm (⅛ in.) smaller than the rabbet size of the frame you have just made. (You may also, of course, cut the mount to fit a particular frame you already have on hand.) Measurements for the mount width are marked on the *back* of the board. Add the rabbet width 6 mm (¼ in.) to the mount width (76 mm [3 in.]) and subtract 2 mm (⅟₁₆ in.) (since mount was cut 3 mm [⅛ in.] smaller than rabbet size). The total (86 mm [3⅜ in.] in this case) is then measured in from edge of board and marked with a small pencil dot. (The extra 5 mm (³⁄₁₆ in.) is the amount of mount that will be covered by the frame.) Place compass pencil on dot and draw towards you as shown in the photograph on page 37.

CUTTING Mounting-knife blades require constant sharpening on a sharpening stone in order to cut clean edges. The lower the quality of board they cut, the quicker they will dull. Avoid cutting corrugated board and chipboard with the same blade used to cut mountboard. Whenever you cut out a mount, place scrap mountboard under the line to be cut to avoid cutting into the table and dulling the blade.

Because the mount knife is held at an angle if you want a bevelled edge, it will seem that you are cutting a fraction more than is really the case. Compensate by cutting a fraction beyond each intersection, but just a fraction. If you cut too much–because you want to be sure–tell-tale lines will show at the corners on the front of the mount.

When the mount is completed, check it from the front. Remove any roughness on the window edges with a light-handed application of fine sandpaper. Be gentle; you are working with cardboard, not wood. Rounded corners can be corrected with the craft knife or a single-edge razor blade. Remove finger smudges or dirt with a kneaded eraser.

5 To cut out window, start a fraction beyond intersecting lines. First cut is very light, just enough to form a shallow groove for the second cut

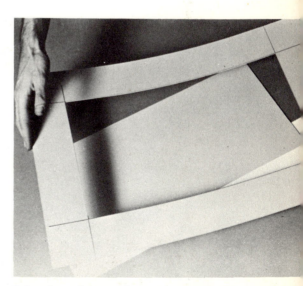

6 Cut from intersection to intersection, but always a fraction beyond. The centre should fall out readily

Fabric Mats

The fabric coverings most preferred for mounts are linen and silk, with linen the better choice for the beginner because it is thicker and therefore easier to manage. If silk should prove too lavish for the picture, smooth fibreboard could be used instead. Burlap, monk's cloth, and grasscloth can be experimented with for their effect on the picture, but remember, they may in time discolour the artwork.

The mount can be cut from inexpensive single-thick grey chipboard or regular mountboard. The main difference between the two is the undertone of colour each lends to the fabric. The fabric should be cut about 50 mm (2 in.) larger than the outside dimensions of the mount. You will also need a brush, white paste, and a single-edge razor blade.

Any bubbling which forms in the fabric after it has been glued to the mat can be remedied with a hot iron. Simply cover the area with a linen or paper patch that is larger than the iron. The bubble should iron out, but if it simply moves, the indication is that air is trapped. In that case, gently lift the fabric until the bubble is reached, cover it with a patch, and iron outwards to edge of mount.

When the fabric mount has been completed, excess glue around the flaps can be covered with strips of paper. It is advisable to use fibrepaper, particularly if the picture is valuable.

1 Mount with fabric cut about 50 mm (2 in.) wider than mount

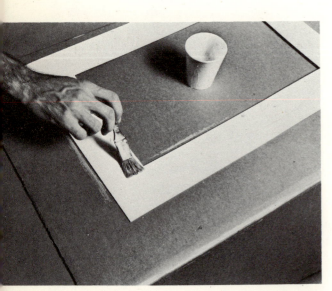

2 Place mount face up. Coat surface, right to edge, thinly but thoroughly with glue. Spread evenly

3 When glue is tacky, position fabric so that its grain is horizontal to shape of mount

4 The fabric should adhere tightly to the mount. Starting at the centre, gently rub with cloth. Work any bubbles out to edges

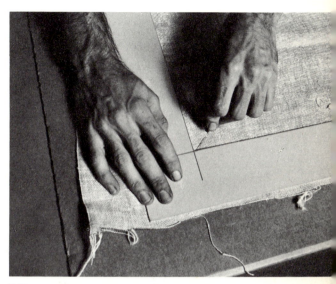

5 To cut out window, turn mount face down. Starting a short distance from each corner, make 25 mm (1 in.) long mitre cut

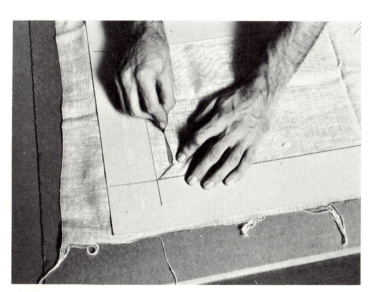

6 Cut straight across from one mitre cut to another

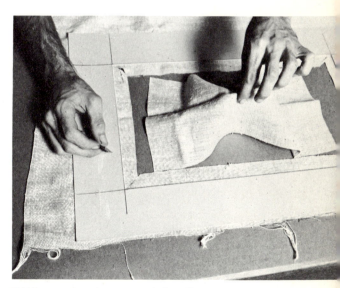

7 When centre is removed, four flaps should remain beyond inside edges of mount window. See next page

8 Apply thin coat of glue, about 25 mm (1 in.) wide (or width of overlap), and allow to get tacky. Be sure there are no glue puddles

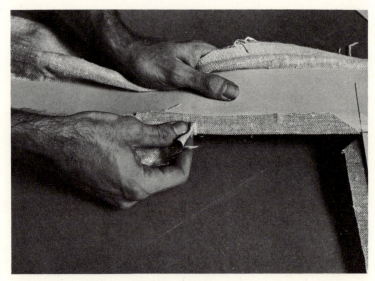

9 To soften flap, rub fabric patch along edge. Start at centre, work towards ends. When soft, rub onto mount surface

10 Turn mount face up and trim off excess fabric at outside edges

11 The fabric mount is now finished, ready to be inserted into a frame

Mounting the Picture

To mount the picture, first place the mount over it and adjust for the right position. Remove mount and keep sight marking in mind. Then tape the picture as shown on the right.

HINGED MOUNT. This type of mount gives added protection to the picture, and is also used for pictures that are not going to be framed. It is made by cutting a second mountboard to the outside dimensions of the mount and taping both together at their top edges.

First place the mounting board face up on the table and the mount face down so that the top of the mount is flush with the top of the mounting board (see diagram on left, below). Wet a piece of gummed paper tape that has been cut a little shorter than the flush sides and place the tape over both where they meet. Fold the mount over the mounting board and adjust them both so that one fits exactly over the other. Press the top edge of the mount to crease the tape. Once the hinged mount is made, the art is taped on or tipped in place. For how to tip the art, see page 45.

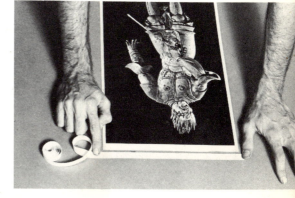

Using linen tape, wet it and slide just under top edge of picture

Press mount onto tape. Rub with cloth for a good bind

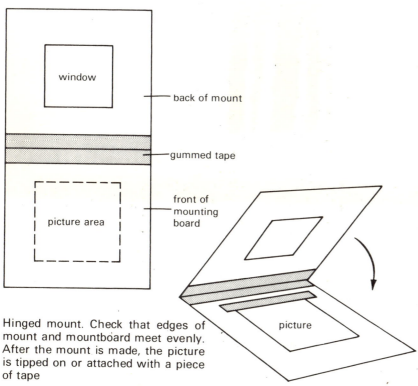

Hinged mount. Check that edges of mount and mountboard meet evenly. After the mount is made, the picture is tipped on or attached with a piece of tape

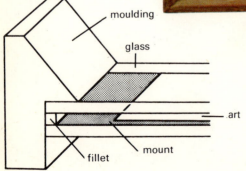

"Girl with Rooster," by Gregorio Prestopino. Serigraph. Mounted on coloured, textured Bainbridge mountboard. Under glass. Frame 794 mm x 648 mm (31¼ in. x 25½ in.), print 660 mm x 508 mm (26 in. x 20 in.), moulding 32 mm (1¼ in.)

Mounts

A mount permits the edges of the paper of the art to show. The picture is tipped on so that the margins of the mounting board form a background. Aesthetically, this produces a starker presentation of the picture than if it were mounted, since a mount creates the illusion of depth. With increasing frequency artwork is being framed in this manner, particularly when the art is on mulberry paper or rice paper, or on other papers with frayed or interesting edges.

Mountboard is commonly employed though once again, if the art is valuable, 100 per cent fibreboard should be used. For a fabric mount, glue the fabric to the board as for a mount (see page 40).

The trickiest part of mounting is situating the picture in the proper place. You may feel certain that it is centred correctly, only to finish it, hang it on the wall, and find out, to your surprise, that it is situated left of centre or is crooked. After you have cut the mount to the desired size, adjust the picture on it until you feel there is an even margin all round.

Your sight markings will probably be a little off. To correct them, place a Tee-square flush with the bottom edge of the picture and measure for the margin from the bottom of the mount to the top of the Tee-square. Move the Tee-square up or down as required until it is parallel with the bottom of the mount. Once the bottom margin is the proper width, the top margin will be corrected automatically. The side to side positions can now be set. To free both hands, place weights on the Tee-square so it won't slip. Measure for the margin from one side of the mount and slide the picture to that point, keeping it on the plane parallel to the bottom of the mount. The other side will be corrected automatically.

The next step is to tip the picture onto the mount. Place a weight on it to keep it in the correct position for gluing. Lift one of the top corners of the picture and apply just a pinhead of glue to the mount under it. Go in a bit from the edges of the picture so that the glue will not show. Do the same for the other top corner. Linen hinges can be used instead of glue. Press down lightly on both corners and allow the glue to dry for about five minutes.

Certificate tipped onto coloured mountboard, hand stippled for textural effect. Glass. An ideal way of giving joy and encouragement to a child.

Liners

Canvases and wooden panels are frequently framed with a liner between the art and the frame. A liner is a wooden moulding, usually covered with fabric, and is to a canvas or panel as a mount is to paper; it serves as a breathing space and prevents the painting from visually crashing into the frame. When framing a canvas or panel, you will probably not need glass. A liner can also be used as a decorative border for pictures. If not fabric-covered, it can be painted or metal-leafed. It also adds dimension to a narrow moulding, and can serve to reduce the size of a frame that is too large for the art.

A liner is made in the same manner as a frame and with the same care. Since its outer sides will fit into the frame rabbet and will not be seen, it is not necessary to counter-sink the nails with a nail set. Sand the liner well, especially at its mitred corners. When it is finished, insert the canvas or panel to check its fit.

Before measuring for the liner, make sure the canvas stretcher is in good shape. If it is sagging, gently hammer the keys in its corners. When measuring, include the canvas folds at each corner. If the stretcher is 406 mm x 508 mm (16 in. x 20 in.), the measure will most likely be closer to 409 mm x 511 mm (16⅛ in. x 20⅛ in.) including the corner canvas folds. Liner rabbet size should be (as should all rabbet sizes) a little larger than that which is going into it. In this case, probably 412 mm x 514 mm (16¼ in. x 20¼ in.).

The frame fits around the liner. Add 3 mm (⅛ in.) to the outside dimensions of the liner for the frame rabbet size. Cut and join the frame as usual, then place it face down and insert the liner, also face down. If the liner fits a little loosely in the frame rabbet, centre it by sliding scrap strips of mountboard between it and the rabbet. Secure the liner to the frame with long brads, angling each brad so that it enters the frame rabbet. It is a good idea to nail through the mountboard strips to keep them from sliding.

Place the canvas face down in the liner. It should fit snugly, but if it fits loosely, centre it with mountboard strips. Using long brads, place the point of each into the wall of the liner, pressing the shaft against the bottom outside of the stretcher. While still pressing, nail the brad into the liner, but not all the way. Leave enough so that it can be hammered to bend over the edge of the stretcher.

Spring clips or mending plates can be used in place of brads. Spring clips, available in art-supply stores, are shaped to hold a canvas in place. Simply screw one end of the clip into the liner and, when that end is secured, the other will press down on the stretcher and hold it in the rabbet. Mending plates are sold in most hardware stores and must be shaped to fit the canvas.

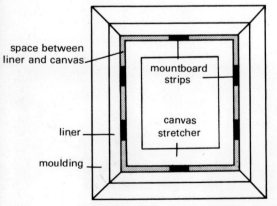

Cover liner with fabric and cut out centre as you would a mount (see page 40). To adhere flaps, lightly apply glue to rabbet on one side. When tacky use scrap material to press fabric over lip and into rabbet. Rub until fabric adheres smoothly. Do other sides. Pay special attention to corners. Trim off excess on outside edges.

Back of framed canvas

If canvas fits loosely in liner, balance scrap strips of mountboard on each side

Gouache. Linen liner with white lip. Glass, A liner provides "breathing space" between the art and the frame. Frame 457 mm (18 in.) square, liner 22 mm (⅞ in.), moulding 32 mm (1¼ in.).

SIMPLE FRAMES

The two examples shown on these pages are of simple framing. One is a needlework and both are under glass. Although these are similar to the framing described in the Basic Frame section–in that they contain just art, glass, and backing–note how dissimilar they are in total effect. The point to keep in mind here is that simple framing can achieve an imposing result.

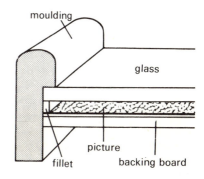

(Facing page) Crewel embroidery, by Elsie Anzalone from an Erica Wilson design. Fabric was stretched onto a strainer before being set into frame. Basswood, stained and waxed. Non-glare glass. Frame 850 mm x 485 mm (34 in. x 19 in.), moulding 83 mm (3¼ in.)

(Below) American Indian print. Print extends to rabbet of frame. Waxed wormwood moulding. Glass. Frame 330 mm x 483 mm (13 in. x 19 in.), moulding 50 mm (2 in.) deep with 19 mm (¾ in.) face

Watercolour, by Arthur Shilstone. Use of double mount. Colours of mountboards were chosen to blend with painting. Glass. Frame 584 mm x 673 mm (23 in. x 26½ in.), mount 76 mm (3 in.), moulding 44 mm (1¾ in.). Collection of Mr and Mrs Stephen Greenwald

FRAMES WITH MOUNTS

Eight examples of the use of mounts are shown on these pages and on the four following. As can be seen, mounts can be simple white, or coloured to accentuate colour in the art, or textured for a rich effect. They can be narrow, or can be doubled and overlapped slightly to add character to the presentation. They can also have multiple openings to display art of a related subject. Note on page 55 that instead of cutting a window large enough to show the title, a separate opening was cut out instead.

(Above) Old fish print. Pale grey mount in a silver-faced frame (brushed silver and gold) harmoniously blend with the greys and blues and fine black lines of the print. Frame 200 mm x 241 mm (7¾ in. x 9½ in.), moulding 12 mm (½ in.), mount 35 mm (1⅜ in.) top and sides, 41 mm (1⅝ in.) bottom

(Left) Ink drawing. White mat on white paper. An effective use of a thin mount. Frame 406 mm x 305 mm (16 in. x 12 in.), mount 25 mm (1 in.)

"Wildflowers," watercolour. Mouldings are in deep neutral tones to dramatize flowers rendered in full colour on white paper. Contemporary Florentine style moulding, stained, then splattered with raw umber and black mixed in alcohol solution. Glass. Frame 508 mm x 559 mm (20 in. x 22 in.), moulding 64 mm (2½ in.)

Hand-coloured prints from old book. The use of coloured mounts adds new interest to old prints.

(Left) Title page from *Naturalist's Library.* Glass. Frame 267 mm x 191 mm (10½ in. x 7½ in.), moulding 10 mm (⅜ in.), mount 38 mm (1½ in.) top and sides, 50 mm (2 in.) bottom

(Below) "Butterflies," an example of three prints in one mount. Same moulding as above. Glass. Frame 292 mm x 470 mm (11½ in. x 18½ in.), mount 50 mm (2 in.) top and sides, 64 mm (2½ in.) bottom, 32 mm (1¼ in.) between prints

Oil painting on paper, by Selina Trief. Thinly applied pigment on paper makes it possible to mount such art and put it under glass. Walnut moulding faced in silver. Frame 330 mm x 406 mm (13 in. x 16 in.), moulding 12 mm (½ in.), mount 76 mm (3 in.)

"H. Prouse Cooper's Downtown Store," *circa* 1880. Watercolour. Note title opening in mount. Frame is inlaid veneer. Glass. Frame 533 mm x 635 mm (21 in. x 25 in.), moulding 89 mm (3½ in.). Collection of Herbert W. Hemphill, Jr

Quick sketch watercolour mounted on dark linen, art tipped on. Natural stain on walnut moulding. Glass. Frame 508 mm x 356 mm (20 in. x 14 in.), moulding 12 mm (½ in.), border 76 mm (3 in.)

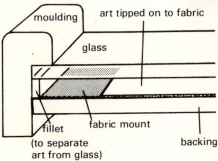

moulding

art tipped on to fabric

glass

fillet
(to separate
art from glass)

fabric mount

backing

FRAMES WITH FABRIC MOUNTS

The effect of solidarity that is created by surrounding the art with fabric is shown in the examples here and on the following four pages. Various media are so treated with fabric-covered mounts. Different textiles can be used, depending upon their sympathy with the subject. Most textiles will provide a neutral but textured background for the art and should blend harmoniously with it.

Engraving. An example of how the textural quality of a fabric mount can add importance to a small-sized print. Sandy linen mount. Gold leaf on gesso, antiqued. Frame 279 mm x 330 mm (11 in. x 13 in.), moulding 38 mm (1½ in.), mount 57 mm (2¼ in.)

A calendar print. Linen fabric mount. Moulding finished with gesso and sprayed with plastic paint (see Finishing for this method). Frame 457 mm x 304 mm (18 in. x 12 in.), mount 76 mm (3 in.)

"Hawk," by Anthony Saris. Ink and crayon. Art is tipped onto mount.
White silk mount. Glass. Frame 622 mm x 552 mm (24½ in. x 21¾ in.),
moulding 25 mm (1 in.). Collection of Mr and Mrs Stephen Greenwald

Wedding photograph. Raw silk on grey mountboard. An example of contemporary framing. Walnut moulding stained. Glass. Frame 584 mm x 483 mm (23 in. x 19 in.), moulding 12 mm (½ in.), mount 76 mm (3 in.)

(Facing page) "Autumn," by S. E. Sayles. Watercolour. Mounted on natural linen. Oak moulding, waxed. Glass. Painting 508 mm x 406 mm (20 in. x 16 in.), frame 650 mm x 558 mm (26 in. x 22 in.), moulding 19 mm (¾ in.)

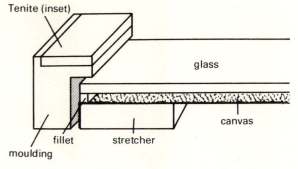

Tenite (inset)

glass

canvas

fillet stretcher

moulding

"Long Life," by Chi Chou Watts. Grass-school calligraphy (Ts-Ao) style. Rice paper mounted on off-white canvas. Moulding opaque white Tenite set into basswood. Glass. Frame 916 mm x 425 mm (40 in. x 16¾ in.), moulding 12 mm (½ in.). Collection of Mr and Mrs William Sayles

FRAMING CANVASES

Four examples of canvases can be seen here and on the next page. A fifth example, on page 65, is of a wood panel, but it is treated for framing in the same manner as a canvas. The same treatment applies to the Chinese calligraphy shown on the left, which was mounted on canvas. The canvases shown are with and without liners, and where the liners appear they are linen covered.

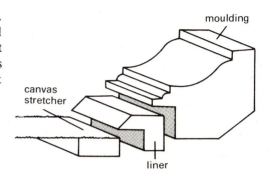

"Still Life," artist unknown. American primitive. Oil, with linen liner. Contemporary Florentine moulding, stained and splattered for toning. Frame 375 mm x 476 mm (14¾ in. x 18¾ in.), moulding 44 mm (1¾ in.), liner 19 mm (¾ in.)

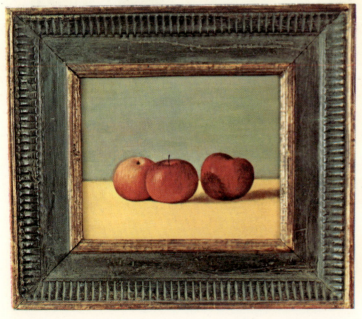

Two paintings by Elsie Manville. Oils. Examples of ornate frames that add a highly decorative quality to simple subjects

(Above) "Acorn Squash." Spanish style frame with linen liner. Gold leaf on gesso with gouache in panel of moulding. Frame 279 mm x 356 mm (11 in. x 14 in.), moulding 64 mm (2½ in.), liner 25 mm (1 in.)

(Left) "Apples,' 18th-century Italian style frame. Gold leaf and gouache on gesso. Frame 229 mm x 330 mm (9 in. x 13 in.), moulding 50 mm (2 in.)

"Oregon," oil painting on wood panel. Framed in same manner as canvas. French Louis XVI style frame. 18th century. Gold leaf on gesso. Frame 330 mm x 229 mm (13 in. x 9 in.), moulding 38 mm (1½ in.). Collection of Mr and Mrs Stephen Manville

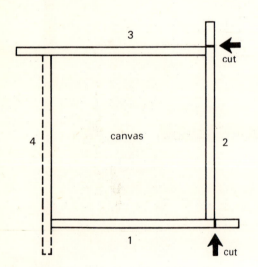

Cut off overhang on 1st and 2nd corners before adding 4th strip.

"Maria," by J. Bostar, Jr. Oil. Baguette frame. The corners of the frame are butted instead of mitred. Gold Tenite on mahogany. Frame 508 mm x 406 mm (20 in. x 16 in.), moulding 38 mm (1½ in.) deep with 8 mm ($\frac{5}{16}$ in.) face

Baguette

A baguette, commonly referred to as "stripping," is a protective strip used in place of a frame, most frequently for canvases. It may be of wood–waxed, painted, or gilded–or have a top surface of Tenite plastic in gold, silver, black, or white. The strips are narrow, about 5 mm to 11 mm ($\frac{3}{16}$ in. to $\frac{7}{16}$ in.) wide by 32 mm to 50 mm (1¼ in. to 2 in.) deep, and do not have a rabbet. Although a baguette can be cut and joined in the same manner as a frame, it is usually nailed flush to the canvas stretcher, one strip at a time, with its corners butted rather than mitred.

You will need four strips, each cut 50 mm (2 in.) longer than the size it will cover. Place them on a flat surface and start brads in each one, spacing them about 127 mm (5 in.) apart. Generally the

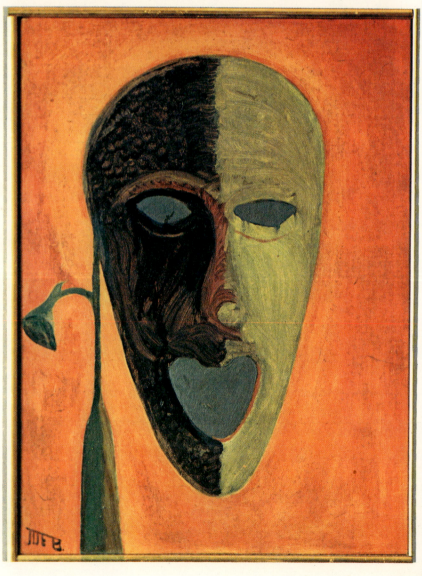

best locations for the brads is just short of centre between the face and the back of the moulding. Do not nail through the wood; the brads should just be fixed in place.

Stand the canvas up, face towards you, and place a flat object, such as a sanding block, along the top of one of its vertical sides so that it protrudes above the horizontal plane of the canvas. Place a baguette strip of the correct length (the length of the side plus 50 mm [2 in.]) on top of the canvas, sliding it up against the block (see diagram on page 66). Its face should protrude beyond the face of the canvas so that, when completed, the canvas will be set back 3 mm to 6 mm (⅛ in. to ¼ in.).

Holding the baguette firm, remove the block. Hammer in the brads, checking after each to make sure the baguette is straight. *Take care that no brads puncture canvas face.* Once the first strip is nailed down, turn canvas so nailed side becomes a vertical side. The protruding 50 mm (2 in.) of baguette can now replace the sanding block as a register guide. Nail this side and third side in the same manner, then return to the first corner. Using very narrow brads, reinforce the two butted ends on that corner. Two brads should be sufficient. Place canvas on edge of table, face towards you, and using the vertical side as guide, saw off excess baguette (see diagram). Repeat on second butted corner. Return to fourth side and nail on that strip. Reinforce the two remaining butted corners, then saw off excess as before. Sand all corners well.

VARIATIONS. The above method is the most common, but variation can be obtained by "floating" the baguette. Beside baguette strips, you will need four strips of fibreboard about 6 mm (¼ in.) shallower than the depth of the canvas and equal in length to its dimensions.

Tape the sides of the canvas with black tape and paint the fibreboard strips black to match. With small brads, nail these strips to the canvas sides, their edges flush with the back of the canvas. They should not reach to the canvas face. Now nail on the baguette as before, being sure to nail into the fibreboard strips. When you are finished, there should appear to be a narrow black void between the canvas and the baguette. Lacking any visual evidence of support, the baguette will appear to be "floating" around the canvas. (See diagram at right.)

A baguette moulding can also be used together with a liner. It is most frequently seen with a wrap-around liner which is made the same way as on page 46, except that instead of the excess fabric on its outside edges being trimmed off, it is wrapped around the sides of the liner (which have first been glued) and then is either glued down in the back or is trimmed off. The baguette is attached to the liner in the same manner as it is to the stretcher of the canvas.

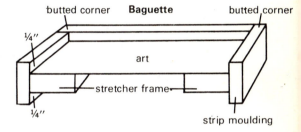

butted corner **Baguette** butted corner
¼″
art
¼″ stretcher frame
strip moulding

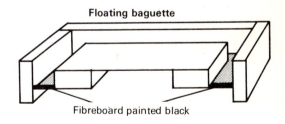

Floating baguette
Fibreboard painted black

Shadow Box

A three-dimensional object can be tastefully and appropriately framed in a setting which will provide sufficient depth for its size. Such a setting, called a shadow box, can be used for objects as diverse as fans, needlework, and miniatures, or for decorative arrangements of medals, coins, and keepsakes.

To establish the minimum depth for the rabbet of the frame, you must first measure the thickness of the object, then allow a small space between its surface and the glass, and a further allowance for the thickness of the glass, the mounting board, and the backing board (optional). Let us assume that you have a small but thickly woven tapestry that you want to mount on silk and then frame. If the tapestry is 6 mm (¼ in.) thick, allow that amount plus a 6 mm (¼ in.) space between it and the glass, then 3 mm (⅛ in.) each for the glass, the mounting board, and the backing board. These measurements added together will give the minimum depth necessary for the frame rabbet–22 mm (⅞ in.) to accommodate all the inserts; 25 mm (1 in.) to do it safely.

Once you have chosen the moulding, the steps are the same as in making the basic frame. After the mount for the tapestry has been covered with fabric (see page 45), the object is glued or sewn onto it to keep it secured. Depending upon the object to be sewn, nylon thread, thin wire, or fishing line can be used. For this tapestry, nylon thread would do. In sewing, be sure to pierce through the mounting board. Sew only the top side of the tapestry, allowing the sides and bottom to hang freely.

FILLETS. When the tapestry has been mounted, place glass in the frame. You will need four fillets (thin strips of wood or Masonite) to hold the glass in place and to form a rabbet for the mount. For this frame, cut the fillets 12 mm (½ in.) wide. Their depth should not be greater than the width of the frame rabbet (see diagram).

Wrap the fillets in the same fabric used to cover the mounting board and glue them neatly in place to the rabbet wall with their narrow edges flush against the glass. When the glue has dried, place the mount with tapestry attached into the rabbet created by the fillet and the frame rabbet wall. Insert the backing and secure the frame as usual.

The shadow box just described is relatively shallow, but boxes can be made as deep as 102 mm to 152 mm (4 in. to 6 in.), either through necessity or taste (see example on facing page). In such instances the box has a depth sufficient to create strong and deep shadows. An effective shadow box can also be made by using a very deep frame and a 76 mm (3 in.) fabric liner behind the glass The art is then set back about 76 mm or 102 mm (3 in. or 4 in.).

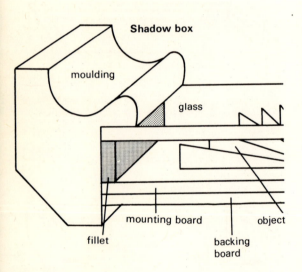

Shadow box

moulding

glass

mounting board

object

fillet

backing board

"May-Flower," *circa* 1890, probably constructed by a sailor in the New York area. Approx. size 356 mm x 508 mm x 152 mm (14 in. x 20 in. x 6 in.) deep. Collection of Mr Herbert W. Hemphill, Jr

Print from the *Nuremberg Chronicles,* 15th century. Placed between two pieces of glass so that it can be viewed from either side. Frame size 416 mm x 433 mm (16⅜ in. x 17¹⁄₁₆ in.). Collection of Mary Walker Phillips

Glass Trap

If you have two pictures, one on each side of the same paper, you may want to frame them so that either side can be viewed. The frame that will suit this purpose perfectly is a glass trap, so called because it has glass on both sides, with the artwork between. This makes it possible to remove the frame from the wall to view the artwork in back.

It is advisable to use a mount whenever you are going to make a glass trap. A mount provides for easier handling of the artwork as well as affording it protection from the two sheets of glass. The mount for a glass trap has to be a double one since both surfaces of the artwork will be viewable.

The procedure for making the frame is the same as for any frame which will hold glass. The difference will come in the fitting. Instead of a backing board, the second piece of glass is used.

Ready the frame and apply a stain finish to its back. Attach the artwork between the two identical mounts. Cut two pieces of glass to fit into the rabbet of the frame and clean them thoroughly. Place the twin mounts and the artwork in between them. Then fit this set into the rabbet of the frame.

You will now need four fillets to fit into the frame (a small frame will not need fillets). They should be cut equal in width to the distance between the outer surface of the back piece of glass and the bottom edge of the frame, as illustrated in the diagram. Glue these fillets neatly in place in the frame.

When the fillets are thoroughly dry, fix the screw eyes in place. Make sure that they are long enough to pierce through the fillets and penetrate into the moulding so that they will be firmly secured. String the picture wire through the screw eyes. The glass trap is now ready to be hung.

OTHER POSSIBILITIES. The back of the frame can be faced with a moulding similar to the one in the front. However, this second moulding should be cut in half so that it will not have a rabbet.

An alternative method is to use two similar frames, cutting off a portion of the rabbet of each so that both provide half the rabbet space necessary. Put the components in between the halves and then glue both halves together to secure.

Glass trap without mounts

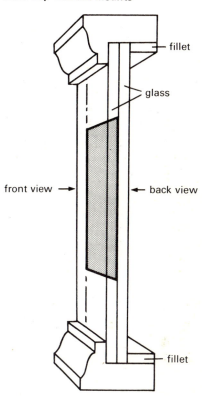

Glass trap with mounts

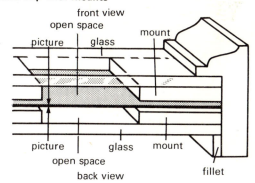

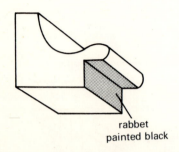

rabbet
painted black

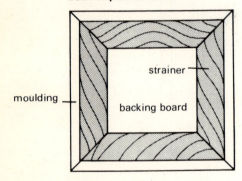

Back of picture frame

strainer

moulding

backing board

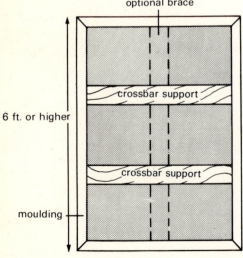

Back support for large mirror

optional brace

crossbar support

6 ft. or higher

crossbar support

moulding

Mirrors

When planning a frame for a mirror, keep one very important point in mind–a mirror is heavy, and requires a strong moulding. It is surprising how the weight of a mirror can come to bear on a picture frame. If you have any doubts as to the ability of the frame to maintain this weight over a long period of time, reinforce it by any of the methods which follow.

These methods can be used even if the mirror is already framed. They are also well suited for any large painting that has to be braced in the frame to alleviate pressure. Wide cracks in the corners of the frame, especially the bottom two corners, are the most easily-seen evidence of such pressures.

Just one more point when making a frame for a mirror–paint the rabbet black so that its reflection will not be conspicuous.

STRAINER. If the mirror frame is relatively small and narrow, you can reinforce it with a strainer. A strainer is a very simple frame, usually made of 25 mm x 50 mm, 25 mm x 76 mm (1 in. x 2 in., 1 in. x 3 in.) or even 25 mm x 102 mm (1 in. x 4 in.) timber stock, which fits into the rabbet of the picture frame.

Cut and join the sides for the strainer just as you would for a frame. It should be measured so that it will fit snugly into the frame rabbet. Fit the picture frame as you would normally, but insert the strainer before taping up the back. For a mirror–especially when the frame is very narrow, 25 mm (1 in.) or less–the frame should be screwed to the supporting strainer. Sink the screws slightly below the surface of the frame moulding and fill the holes with wood filler. Then tape up the back.

Generally speaking, if you are framing a picture and the moulding is narrow, about 25 mm (1 in.), and any dimension of the frame is over 610 mm (24 in.), you should consider a strainer. Instead of screws, you can use brads, nails, or staples, whichever is best suited.

CROSSBARS. Another way to reinforce a frame against heavy pressure is through the use of crossbars. These are simply strips of wood, again usually 25 mm x 50 mm, 25 mm x 76 mm, or even 25 mm x 102 mm (1 in. x 2 in., 1 in. x 3 in., or even 1. in. x 4 in.), depending upon the size of the frame and the weight to be supported. They are placed across the back of the frame to hold opposite sides firmly parallel to each other. Sometimes they are crisscrossed. Other times, particularly with a narrow moulding with large dimensions, they are used in combination with a strainer.

When crossbars are placed to reinforce the horizontal sides, they alleviate the pressure on one side, usually the bottom. This prevents the moulding from warping out of shape. When the bars are placed to reinforce the vertical sides (see diagram at bottom of page 72), they alleviate the pressure on the corner joints by redistributing it throughout the whole frame structure.

HANGING. If the mirror, or large painting, is larger than 508 mm x 610 mm (20 in. x 24 in.), it would be a good idea to use four screw eyes, two on each side of the frame, as shown in the diagram at the right.

There are special hanging devices for framed mirrors and similar heavy frames. They are called mirror hangers and are available in most art-supply and hardware stores.

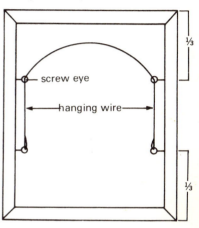

Wiring for heavy framed mirror

— screw eye

— hanging wire —

⅓

⅓

back of framed mirror

Mirror. 17th-century Spanish style frame. Gold leaf on gesso with scraffito in corners of moulding panel. Although traditionally framed, piece is effective in contemporary setting. Frame 610 mm x 508 mm (24 in. x 20 in.), moulding 140 mm (5½ in.)

Passe Partout

Passe partout is a quick, inexpensive, and easy method of protecting a picture for temporary purposes of display, or for the more permanent framing of small pictures or snapshots. There is no actual frame involved, but the tape which is used to bind the edges provides the illusion of one.

In this method the glass, backing, and mount, if used, are cut to size in the usual manner and are held together by strips of tape binding the edges. A hinged mount could also be used here. The picture is hung by means of hangers, called passe partout rings, which are inserted into slits in the backing board and then taped down (see diagram). Special tapes for the binding are available in various colours at art-supply stores, but any tape will do. Just paint it the desired shade.

Once the rings are through the backing board–they should not touch the art–assemble the parts just as you would for fitting a frame. It is important to have all edges evenly aligned.

Allow one edge of this set to project over the edge of the table. Cut a piece of binding tape about 50 mm (2 in.) longer than the side you will first work on. Carefully lay one half of the tape's width along the glass, maintaining an even border all the way across. Press the tape down firmly by rubbing it with your fingernail. Rub it along the edge, then press it to the backing board. Repeat for the opposite side.

Repeat for other two sides. Either mitre or overlap the tape where it meets at the corners and trim off excess. Run picture wire through the passe partout rings and the picture is ready for hanging.

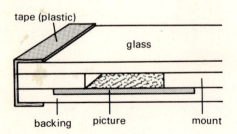

"Poppy Talk", poppy petals on rice paper. Example of non-frame framing. Passe partout. Transparent adhesive 12 mm (½ in.) tape is used to hold the components together. Glass

tape (plastic)

glass

backing   picture   mount

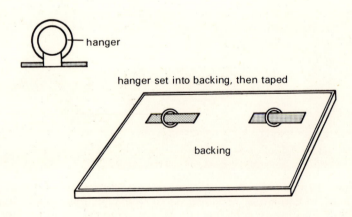

hanger

hanger set into backing, then taped

backing

(Right) Pencil sketch on vellum paper in white mount is framed by brown plastic 19 mm (¾ in.) tape. Size 350 mm x 500 mm (14 in. x 20 in.). Glass

(Below) Mexican gouache on wood fibre. Art is glued onto a blue mounting board. Plastic 12 mm (½ in.) tape binds edges together including glass

Mounting Photographs

If you have a photograph that you want to frame and possibly mount, it is advisable to do the mounting first. When it is mounted correctly it will not wrinkle or buckle, and there will also be less likelihood of it being damaged during handling. There are two methods of mounting photographs: dry mounting and wet mounting. If you prefer not to do the mounting yourself, most commercial photography laboratories or picture-frame shops will do it for you. The wet mounting method can be used for artwork also, but since, during mounting, the picture is adhered completely to a mountboard, you must consider whether it will be benefited by this method. If the picture, particularly a print, has value, mounting could decrease its worth.

DRY MOUNTING is easily done if you have a dry mounting press as shown. If not, a household iron can be used, but with care. You will also need a mountboard, white paper, and dry mounting tissue, all larger than the photograph. The heavier the paper, the more protection it will give to the photograph when it is being ironed. Dry mounting tissue is available at photography-supply stores. As usual you should work on a clean, flat surface such as a tabletop.

Place the mountboard on the table with the photograph face down over it, and the mounting tissue over the back of the photograph. Do not leave any edges uncovered. Allow the iron to get hot and

1 Cover back of photograph with dry mounting tissue. Using heated tacking iron, adhere tissue to photograph at centre. Trim tissue 2 mm ($\frac{1}{16}$ in.) smaller than photograph all around.

just touch its tip to a spot in the centre of the tissue. The heat should adhere the tissue to the photograph. Test the temperature of the iron on a piece of tissue first; if it is too hot, you will know it. The correct temperature is 177°C (350°F), or the setting for linen. Now place the photograph face up on some scrap mountboard and trim off the excess tissue with a single-edge razor blade.

Next the photograph is adhered to the mountboard. Cover the face of the photograph with the white paper and touch the iron to its centre. Iron out towards the edges, pressing down hard. All strokes should be as symmetrical as possible–if you iron from the centre to the top in one stroke, the next stroke should be from centre to bottom. The reason for ironing from the centre outwards is to avoid trapping air, which would cause bubbles to form under the surface of the photograph. When finished, the photograph should be absolutely flat. Either leave a border to achieve a mount effect or trim mountboard so its edges are even with those of the photograph.

WET MOUNTING is so called because the mountboard and the back of the photograph must be wet with a thin but thoroughly applied coat of white glue. When both surfaces are almost dry, place one over the other and cover the face of the photograph with the white paper. Avoid getting glue on the face of the photograph. Iron in the same manner as for dry mounting and trim off the excess board.

2 Place photograph face up on mountboard and tack at opposite corners to prevent possible shifting

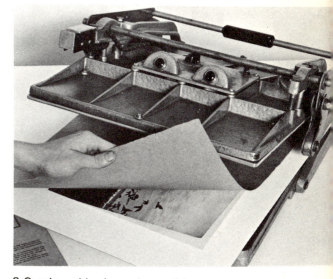

3 Overlay with clean sheet of heavy bond paper larger than photograph. Insert into dry mounting press and lower the heated plate (approx 15 seconds at 177°C (350°F))

Restoring

Many of the older frames to be found today at auctions or at secondhand or antique shops are from the late 19th or early 20th centuries. They are usually metal-leafed or gilded with gold leaf, more frequently the former. And it is not unusual to find the original finish covered by a dull coat of gold paint indicating that some previous owner had found reason to refinish it. Such frames were bright gold when new and their present dull appearances come from age and dirt. The dullness that comes from dirt can be dispelled to some extent, but the dullness of age is there to remain. The only way to separate the effects of dirt from age is to clean the frame with acetone and a stiff brush, both available at a paint supply store.

to clean

Pour some acetone into a bowl or cup, dip the brush in until saturated, then flow the acetone onto a small section (about 76 mm or 102 mm (3 in. or 4 in.)) of the frame. Patiently work the acetone in with the brush, making use of its stiff bristles to get into the crevices of the carving. With a soft absorbent rag occasionally dab the area dry of acetone so you can see how the job is progressing.

Acetone will remove dirt, lacquer, and other sealers without harming the gold itself. The cleaning will heighten or expose the gold. It will, however, remove gold paint. After cleaning the entire frame, permit it to dry. It will do so quickly. Then protect it by sealing its surface with a thin coat of lacquer.

Refinished moulding. By applying a coat of gesso and adding touches of brown and green to accent the colours of the painting, a brighter effect has been achieved

In the cleaning process you may have removed dirt that took fifty to one hundred years to collect, and you may now discover that the frame exhibits extreme wear in spots. Here and there it may even be chipped. An attempt can be made to undo this damage–but remember that such evidence of age is part of the frame's charm.

to refinish

If some of the carvings are very chipped or are missing, and you feel that the frame is still worth your effort, you can try to make its appearance more uniform by additional chipping or by knocking off some ornaments in a more or less symmetrical pattern. The frame can then be sanded or filed roughly or rubbed down with steel wool. You can apply gesso, re-gild, or even paint it. The idea is to experiment for the best effect. You may even have to compromise by cleaning some areas as well as possible and patching up others. With loving care, it should not come off too badly.

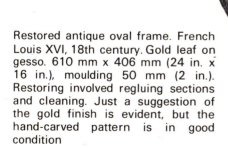

Restored antique oval frame. French Louis XVI, 18th century. Gold leaf on gesso. 610 mm x 406 mm (24 in. x 16 in.), moulding 50 mm (2 in.). Restoring involved regluing sections and cleaning. Just a suggestion of the gold finish is evident, but the hand-carved pattern is in good condition

Suppliers

Frame mouldings and equipment
Handicrafts Limited
Peterborough
Northants
catalogue available

Adhesives, mouldings, passe partout
Fred Aldous Limited
37 Lever Street, Manchester M60 1UX

Paints, gold leaf, passe partout, adhesives, kits
Winsor and Newton Limited
Wealdstone
Harrow
Middlesex
and branches

Fibreboard and liquid stains
available from most hardware stores

Mounting boards, craft knives, adhesives
E. J. Arnold
Butterley Street
Leeds LS10 1AX

Other titles available in the Pan Craft Series:
MACRAMÉ, POTTERY and RUGMAKING (published simultaneously with this volume). To be published in 1973:
JEWELLERY, WEAVING.